TALL, SLIM & ERECT: PORTRAITS OF THE PRESIDENTS

ALEX FORMAN

TrenchArt: Recon

Les Figues Press
Los Angeles

Art (cover) by Renee Petropoulos, "Among Nations - Installment Two (Forman)" and "Language as Form: Displacement 0:02"

Tall, Slim & Erect: Portraits of the Presidents
FIRST EDITION

ISBN 13: 978-1-934254-31-8
ISBN 10: 1-934-254-32-0
Library of Congress Control Number: 2011938226

Les Figues Press thanks its members for their ongoing support and readership. Les Figues Press is a 501c3 organization. Donations are tax-deductible.

The Press would like to acknowledge the following individuals for their generosity: Peter Binkow, Johanna Blakley, Chris and Diane Calkins, Pam Ore, Coco Owen, Mary Swanson.

Les Figues Press titles are available through:
Les Figues Press, <http://www.lesfigues.com>
Small Press Distribution, <http://www.spdbooks.org>

Special thanks to: Emma Williams and Chris Hershey-Van Horn.

TrenchArt 6/2

Book 3 of 5 in the TRENCHART Recon Series.

This project is supported in part by a generous grant from the National Endowment of the Arts.

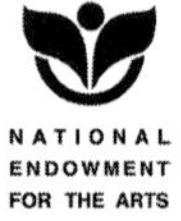

LES FIGUES PRESS
Post Office 7736
Los Angeles, CA 90007
info@lesfigues.com
www.lesfigues.com

There are only old toys with new twists.

– Louis Marx, "The Toy King"

CONTENTS

THE GREAT WORLD IN MINIATURE[1]: AN INTRODUCTION

They are stiff little men, and shiny. They stand alone in empty rooms. They stand pinned, exhibiting themselves, confronting or evading us. Franklin Pierce plays an old cocktail party trick and pretends he's spotted an acquaintance behind us—"You there, hullo!" Clever Andrew Jackson has rendered himself transparent. For his safety, he spawns a double. Lincoln turns his back. Some of them look so afraid! Garfield, McKinley, and Kennedy had reason to ball their fists, but look at Washington, Jefferson, Van Buren, Taylor, Buchanan, Johnson (the first one: Andrew), Cleveland, Nixon. They look terrified. John Quincy Adams is backed into a corner. Warren Harding hides behind a wall. Why do they so mistrust us? We are only watching. They are only being seen.

Who are these little men? They are presidents. American presidents. Great men, huge men. Men of power, audacity and violence. The mightiest men of their day, some of them. (Look at cocky A-Bomb Harry Truman: How big is it? Yay big. It hangs down past my knee.) They are titans. Enormities. Each one only 60 mm tall. They are tiny playthings. Children's toys. Stiff-spined, but you could melt them with a Zippo lighter. You could strap bottle rockets to their legs and shoot them high into the treetops. These are not the presidents you learned about on endless, dreary, grammar school afternoons. They are Alex Forman's presidents, which means, first and foremost, that they are Marxist presidents. Not Karl but Louis Marx: "roly-poly" and "melon-bald,"[2] friend to Dwight

---

1. Cf. John Adams: "In this little state I can discover all the great geniuses, all the surprising actions and revolutions of the great world in miniature." As quoted by Alex Forman in "Ars Poetica," *TrenchArt: Recon.* (Los Angeles: Les Figues Press, 2010). Page 62.

2. Ibid. page 60. That's Alex quoting *Time* magazine of December 12, 1955.

Eisenhower, manufacturer of fine, injection-molded toys. Marx mass-produced plastic figurines of, among other curiosities, cowboys, wild beasts and royals. And of our own beastly cowboy royalty, these 36 miniature heads of state. Men who were monstrously large, brought down to size by Mr. Marx's machinery and now swollen again, reinvested with life and girth by Ms. Alex Forman's lens.

They look so lonely! Nothing to do but be seen. All day, to stand and wait, to be gazed upon, to wait some more. A Beckettian business, the presidency. Yet they're not quite passive. They stare back. Most of them do. They see and they are seen. Which makes them almost… human. And this is at least part of the point. In a prefatory note, the artist writes regarding the text of *Tall, Slim & Erect*: "I have chosen what sentences or paragraphs *humanize* the Presidents' portraits and stories." [italics mine] A perplexing notion, to humanize. Conventionally, we use the word in a semi-Platonic fashion: to indicate the soul of someone; their striving, hurting core; some transcendent portion to which we can all lay claim. But that is not what Alex appears to have in mind. She is asking here what a portrait might be. She is stretching the bounds of the frame and in so doing, posing its contents as questions. What are they—these little presidents, their images, these things called human beings? And what is the polity their persons represent? (i.e. what are we, or at least those 'merikans among us?) With few exceptions—Truman's insomniac aloneness, Lyndon Johnson's hunger for just "a little love"—she informs us primarily of her subjects' kinks, the presidents' corporeal oddities, the idiosyncracies of their appetites, their deaths. Save through compositional and gestural allusion—Lincoln's turned back, wheelchair-bound Franklin Roosevelt standing tall—the great and awful deeds for which they are renowned are for the most part omitted. We learn instead that George Washington had "tremendous" feet and pockmarked cheeks. Adams suffered from "Fidgets, Pidlings" and a crippling "Quiveration" of the hand. Jefferson had boils on his buttocks. John Quincy Adams was a drunk, and flatulent.[3] Andrew Jackson was a slobberer. As an adult at least, no one ever saw Grant naked. Chester Arthur preferred to be dressed by little

3. This may explain his retreat to the rightmost edge of the frame.

boys. During the final weeks of his life, James Garfield took his meals through his rectum. Woodrow Wilson's "ugliness obsessed him." Teddy Roosevelt could eat a whole chicken in a sitting. His cousin, Franklin D., was anorexic but could carry books with his teeth. Upsy-downsy John Fitzgerald Kennedy gobbled speed, taking the edge off with goofballs and paregoric. Chastity caused him headaches. Nixon breakfasted on cottage cheese and ketchup. Tyler died of biliousness and Polk of diarrhea. If there's a humanism at work here, it seems a Rabelaisian one. We are joined by our bodies, their differences as well as what they share. Even presidents fart and itch and fuck. They are not so far away, these tiny giant men. They are separated from us only by the black frame surrounding each photo and by the flatness of each page.

But that distance, however close, is an eternity. Just try and break through it, to push past the surface of the paper, to reach in, to test William Henry Harrison's dread "wilted petunia" grip. In that regard, we'd be fools to forget that the texts Alex uses to describe her presidents are not hers, which is to say (naïvely), that they are borrowings, samplings, collage. They are not written so much as assembled from many dozens of other sources, the ones we deem "original."[4] Her photos undertake a parallel refraction. We are not looking at men but images, digital prints in two dimensions of three-dimensional resinous plastic figurines which were themselves modeled on two-dimensional images in Kodachrome or tintype, daguerrotype or oil. They are quotes of quotes of quotes of quotes, like all of us.

The same could be said—and is here said by inference—about that vast, befuddling abstraction which each of these small men at one point agreed to represent: the nation. And particularly this nation, this boldly self-declared republic (this res publica, or, crudely, this public thing), this grand and mythical democracy. What counts as public? Who gets to be the demos? Throw quotes around "us" too, for "we" are equally citations, remembrances of cropped images drawn from recollections of half-invented

---

4. See bibliography, below, and, if you wish to engage in further research, consult the bibliographies of all works cited there for the sources of the sources. Repeat. Eventually, perhaps, you will reach the great original. "'I' am the selective process," Alex writes. Ibid. page 69.

stories about rumors someone whispered in someone else's ear. Someone perhaps distracted by drunkenness or solitude, by headaches caused by want of intimacy, by burning boils on the buttocks. This does not mean we're nothing. It means we're not finished, never were.

I emailed Alex to ask her about her presidents' feet: where they were, why we could not see them, why she had chosen to uniformly crop them out. (Again: "'I' am the selective process.") She responded: "I was trying to make each president as human as possible. I took them off their pedestals." She was punning: each of Louis Marx's toy statuettes stands on a trapezoidal base. If you look close, you can almost make out Lincoln's. But there's that word again: human. And if I understand her correctly, Alex meant not just that she wished to render her presidents humble and alive, to free them from their frozen iconicity. The naturalist illusion here, such as it is, requires that we not be permitted to glimpse the pedestals, the sight of which would require us to acknowledge that these great and many presidents were naught but children's toys, that they were mere quotes of quotes of quotes, not presidents but precedents. If it is anything, to be human, she suggests, is not only to fart and itch and fuck, but to be complicit in one's own deception, to believe against all better judgment in the accuracy of mirrors. The human is a hole. It is the secret hole in the roof of Grover Cleveland's mouth and the removable rubber stopper he used to plug it up. The nation is a crater. "Take linearity out of history and you get humanity," Alex writes.[5] You get seeing and being seen. You get blindness and invisibility also, words that can be read but often aren't, photos that stare back at you, looping technologies of re-presentation, "an endless tracing,"[6] letters missing, feet left out. Watch carefully. The great are tiny, the miniscule immense.

Ben Ehrenreich
Los Angeles, 2011

5. Ibid. page 67

6. That's me quoting Alex quoting Couze Venn. Ibid. page 70.

TALL, SLIM & ERECT: PORTRAITS OF THE PRESIDENTS

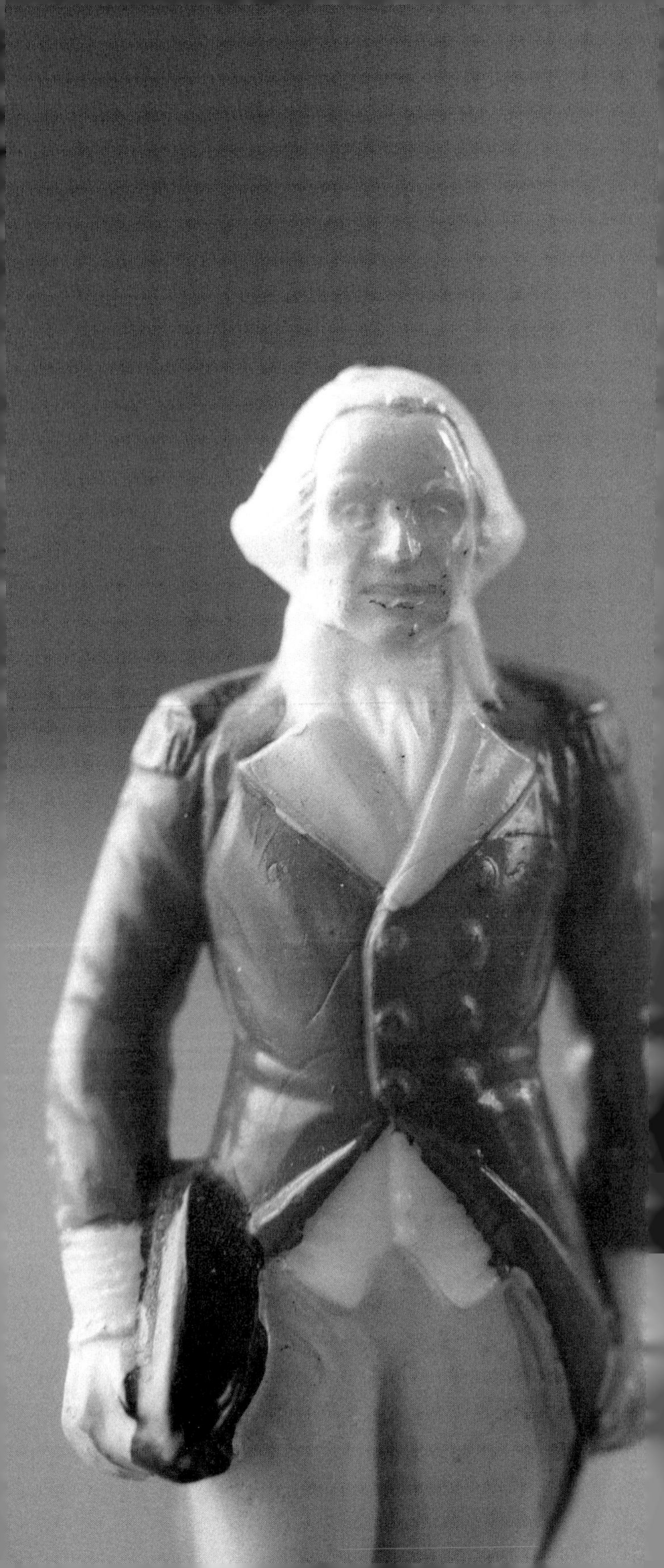

WASHINGTON

1st, 1789–97

Very tall for his generation with reddish hair and gray-blue eyes, George Washington had shoulders too narrow for his height but hands and feet that were tremendous. His face was massive, scarred, and pockmarked.

Gilbert Stuart painted Washington in 1796. Stuart said Washington's features were indicative of the strongest and most ungovernable passions, the sockets of the eyes, for instance, were larger than what I ever met with before, and the upper part of the nose broader. In other words, he had a terrible temper but held it under wonderful control.

With something like a smile, Washington replied, He's right. He said, I am so hackneyed to the touches of the painter's pencil, that I am now altogether at their beck; and sit, like Patience on a monument, whilst they are delineating the lines of my face. At first I was as impatient at the request, and as restive under the operation, as a colt is of the saddle. Now, no dray-horse moves more readily to his thill than I to the painter's chair.

We can safely assume Washington got some schooling between the ages of seven and eleven, and that he did not go on. His 900-volume library was filled with all the get-rich-quick handbooks of the day.

Although Washington was physically strong, he was not the indomitable human force that popular history paints. He was often sick, particularly with infections. Many of them were life threatening, including diphtheria, malaria, smallpox, tuberculosis, and dysentery.

Martha never became pregnant during her forty-year marriage to The Potomac Stallion. Given her previous fertility, it could well be concluded that the difficulty was in her husband. However, Washington, the magnificent athlete, who possessed in abundance every other physical prowess, could not altogether admit to himself that he was sterile.

The bleedings inflicted by Washington's doctors hastened his end. About 35 percent of the blood in his body was drained in twelve hours. His final words were,

Doctor, I die hard; but I am not afraid to go. I am just going. After his death, Washington's frozen corpse measured 6 feet 3 1/2 inches. Doctors hoped Washington was in a suspended state from which he could be aroused: the body would be thawed gradually, first in cool water and then with warm blankets and rubbing of the skin, and finally, a transfusion of lamb's blood.

d. December 14, 1799 (Mount Vernon, Virginia), at 67, from a rare tracheal infection.

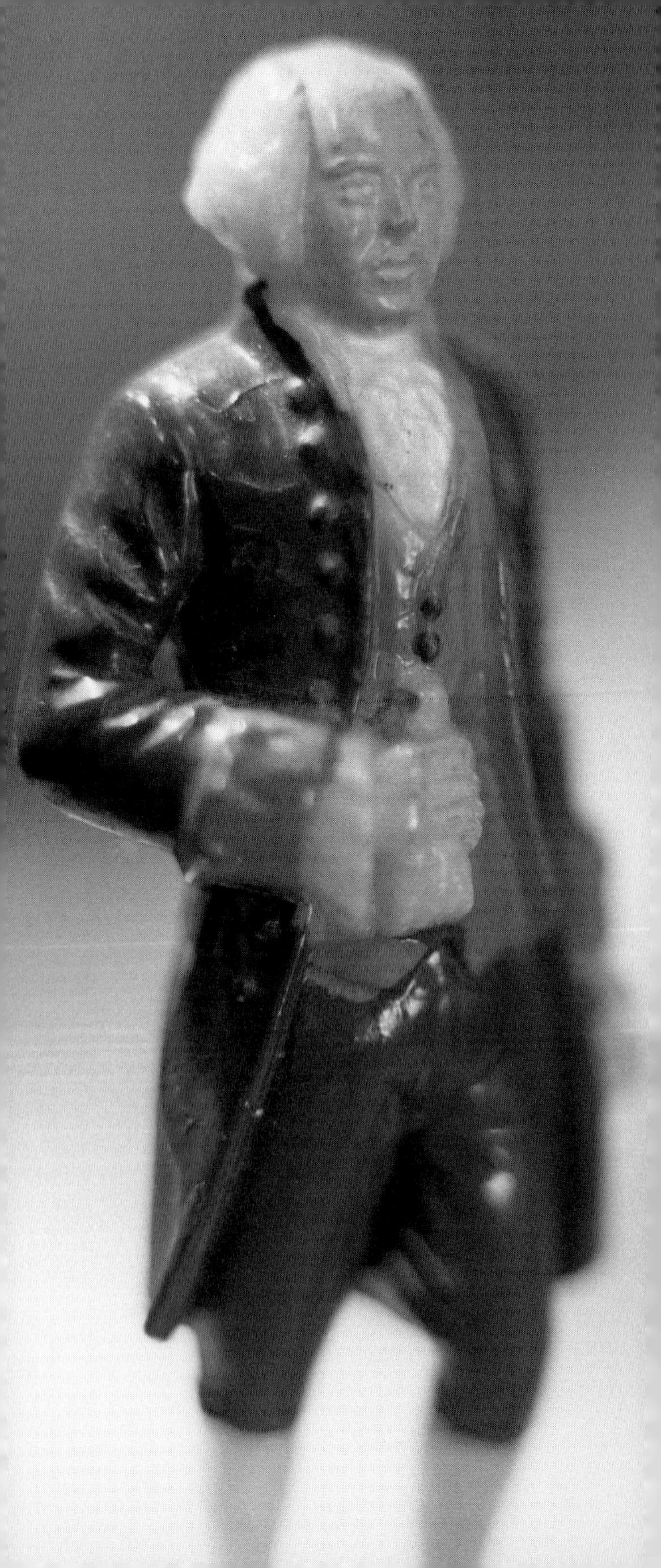

JOHN ADAMS

2nd, 1797–1801

John Adams was not a happy president. He has been labeled manic-depressive, slightly paranoid, and a man consumed by an irrepressible urge to master the world.

Adams started smoking and chewing tobacco at age eight and continued throughout his life.

Once, when asked to provide a physical description of himself, he wrote back: I have one head, four limbs, and five senses, like any other man, and nothing peculiar in any of them. Standing 5 feet 7 inches, Adams was always stocky but grew notoriously plump and was called His Rotundity behind his back.

In Adams's time, political candidates were listed together on a ballot that did not differentiate between the offices. Each elector voted twice, and the highest and next-highest vote getters became president and vice president. Adams liked the system, claiming it would remind great men aspiring to political office the virtues of humility, patience, and moderation, without which every man in power becomes a ravenous beast of prey.

Throughout his life, he was haughty, condescending, self-righteous, and cantankerous; he was so aloof that even the people with whom he joined forces were not always sure he was on their side. To his wife, Abigail, he would address letters My Diana, after the Roman goddess of the moon. He was her Lysander, Spartan hero, giant of great heart.

Adams knew his health deteriorated under stressful circumstances. His diary records: Great Anxiety and distress, and Pain in my Breast and a complaint in my Lungs. His life, he wrote, is a continual Scaene of Fatigue, Vexation, Labour, and Anxiety. Sensitive to heat, he sweated profusely even on cool evenings. He also confessed to Mental Confusion, Fidgets, Pidlings, and Irritabilities.

He said, Ballast is what I want. I totter with every breeze.

The presidency wore out Adams. His eyes weakened so that he could barely read or write, he lost his hair and teeth and he lisped because he refused to wear false ones. He also developed a hand tremor he referred to as Quiveration.

One of two presidents to sign the Declaration of Independence, Adams died on its fiftieth anniversary. His friend and political rival, Jefferson, had died some hours earlier that same day. Although it is said that Adams's last words were *Thomas Jefferson survives,* in fact, the last word was indistinct and imperfectly uttered.

d. July 4, 1826 (Quincy, Massachusetts), at 90, of old age.

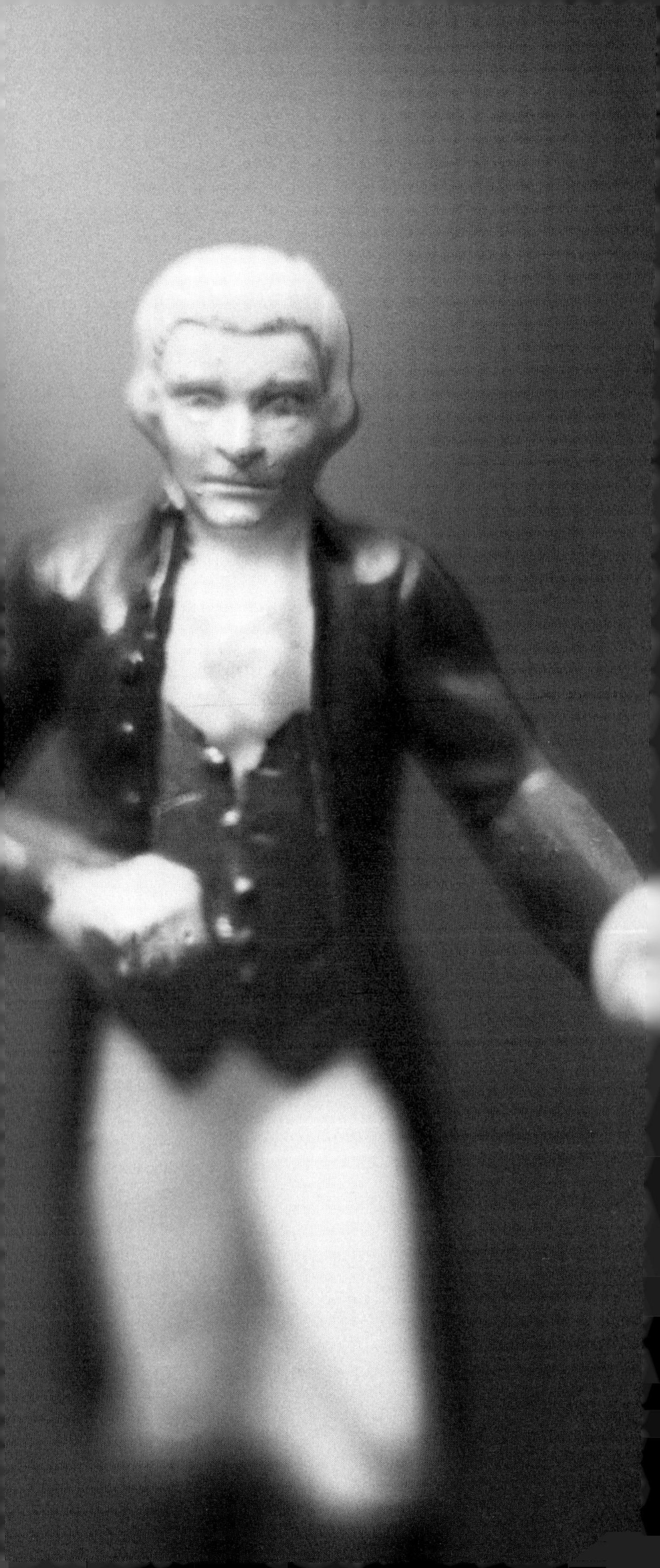

JEFFERSON

3rd, 1801–09

The tall, auburn-haired, hazel-eyed, sharp-featured Thomas Jefferson spoke for the masses and despised what he called the Aristocracy of Wealth. He owned some two hundred slaves, a large plantation, and the grandest house in Virginia. He declared all men to be created equal. He made an exception for African slaves on the ground they weren't people. On a series of dramatic contradictions, a nation was conceived.

A gangling, freckled sloucher and lounger, he opened his doors at the White House to all without regard to social classification. He started the custom of a president shaking hands, rather than bowing to greet guests, and came and went like any other citizen.

He ate little animal meat. Vegetables were his principal diet.

Jefferson suffered from prolonged, incapacitating headaches. These correlated with stress or grief and were complicated by indecision and deeply buried rage. Horseback riding offered relief. In 1818, he had a severe attack of rheumatism. It was accompanied by life-threatening constipation. Jefferson developed boils on his buttocks. For several weeks he conducted his correspondence lying down. He did not ride a horse for several months.

Jefferson spent twenty-five years building his dream house, Monticello, where he brought his bride, the twenty-four-year-old Martha Wayles Skelton, in 1772. Ten years later, as she lay dying, he promised her that he would never remarry, and he never did.

Jefferson made a compilation of the Philosophy of Jesus known as the *Jefferson Bible*. He described it as a paradigma of his doctrines, made by cutting the texts out of the book and arranging them on the pages of a blank book, in a certain order of time or subject.

His *Garden Book* records his love affair with perfection, failure, and renewal. In 1822, he could walk only to reach his garden, and that with sensible fatigue.

He wrote, but though I am an old man, I am but a young gardener. Jefferson became comatose on July 2, 1826. On July 3, he awakened and asked: *Is it the fourth*? He died the next day in virtual poverty, and the house at Monticello, with all its furnishings, was sold to satisfy his creditors.

d. July 4, 1826 (Monticello near Charlottesville, Virginia), at 83, of old age.

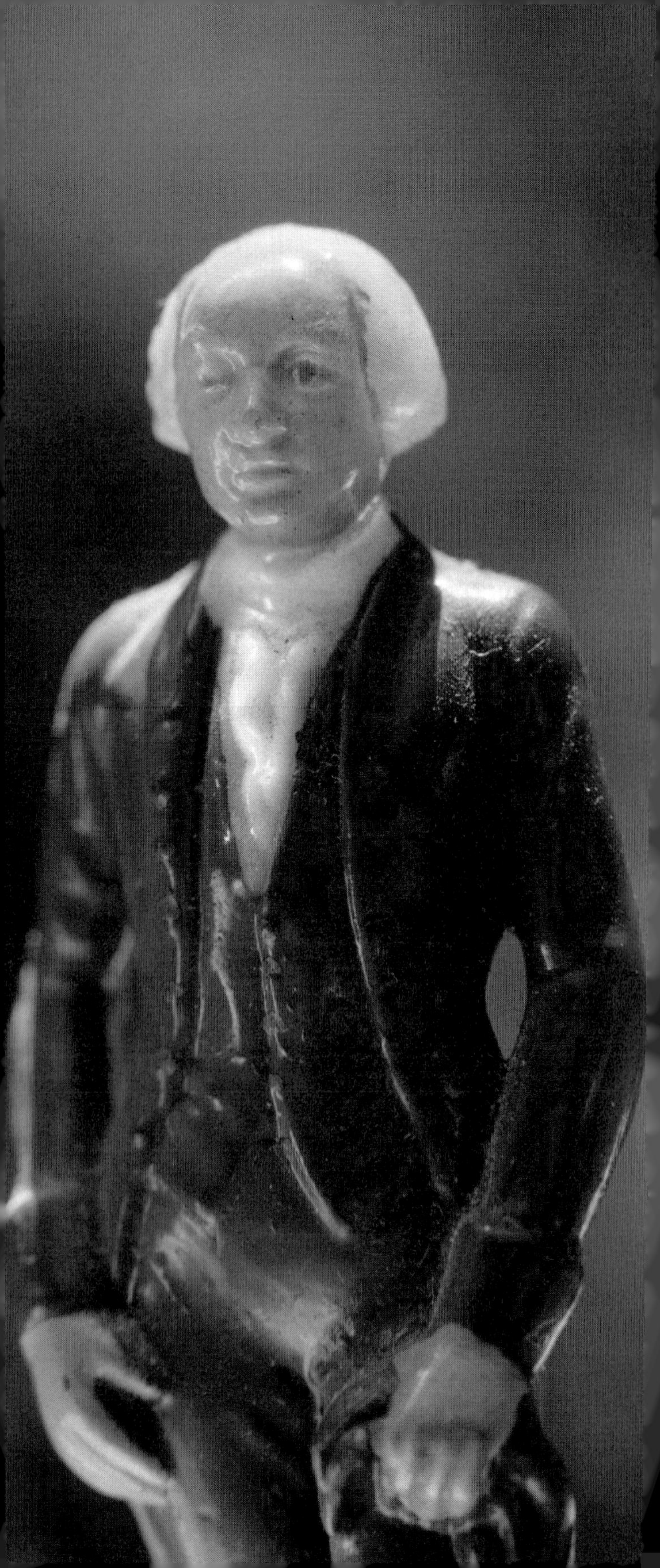

MADISON

4th, 1809–17

James Madison was our smallest president, standing only 5 feet 4 inches and weighing about 100 pounds. An unprepossessing figure—more of a mind than a man—he had a tiny, almost inaudible voice.

This withered little apple-John was the father of the Constitution. He fought the British and Napoleon.

On August 24, 1814, the British torched the Capitol. Madison was a refugee in the hills, and his wife, Dolley, too, had to make a run for it. She hurriedly grabbed everything of value she could, including the Gilbert Stuart portrait of George Washington.

Paul Jennings, a slave born on Madison's estate in 1799, wrote: I was always with Mr. Madison till he died, and shaved him every other day for sixteen years. He was very neat, but never extravagant, in his clothes. He always dressed wholly in black—coat, breeches, and silk stockings, with buckles in his shoes and breeches.

Madison's nose was scarred from frostbite. He claimed it was a wound received in defense of his country.

Chronic arthritis afflicted Madison from middle age onwards. In a letter to James Monroe, dated April 21, 1831, he wrote: In explanation of my microscopic writing, I must remark that the older I grow the more my stiffening fingers make smaller letters, as my feet take shorter steps; the progress in both cases being, at the same time, more fatiguing as well as more slow.

By his early eighties, Madison started to fade away. His vision and his hearing deteriorated, and he grew thinner and weaker. During his final illness, he refused the requests of friends to take stimulants in order to prolong his life until the Fourth of July. On his deathbed he said to his wife, *Nothing but a change of mind, my dear.*

Madison was found dead in his bedroom, sitting in front of his untouched breakfast tray.

d. June 27, 1836 (Montpelier, Vermont), at 85, of old age.

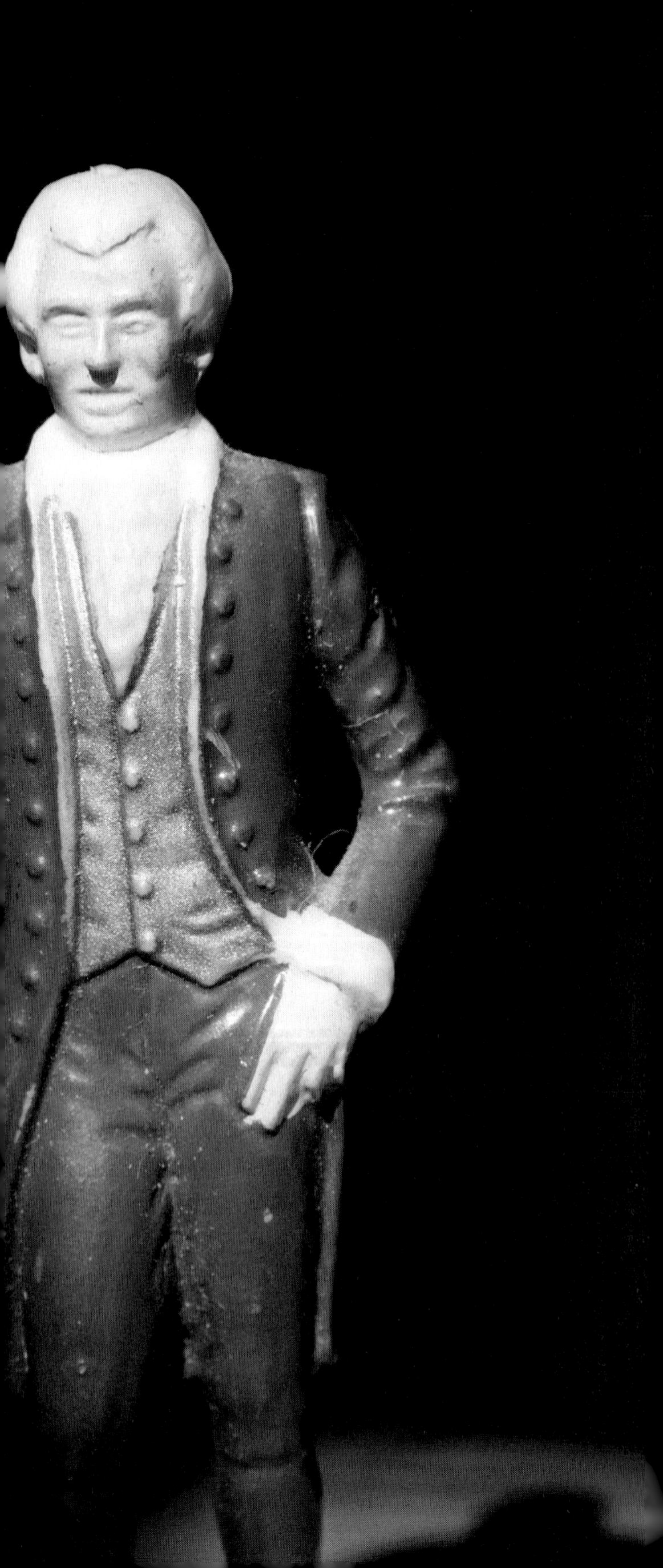

MONROE

5th, 1817–25

James Monroe, a lanky, blue-eyed, commonplace man of no great brilliance, was the last president to wear knee breeches. He stood tall, angular, erect, his features large and chiseled, and from a short distance he bore an unmistakable resemblance to George Washington.

So serene and successful was his eight-year administration that it was known as the Era of Good Feeling.

Less is known about Monroe's thoughts on religion than those of any other president. In his first inaugural address, he praised religious freedom, boasting that Americans may worship the Divine Author in any manner they choose. Thomas Paine wrote *The Age of Reason* in Monroe's home in Paris. Monroe was a Freemason.

In private, Monroe and his wife, Elizabeth, spoke only in French.

Despite earning $25,000 a year as president, Monroe left the White House $75,000 in debt. In "The Memoir of James Monroe, Exqr., relating to his Unsettled Claims upon the People and the Government of the United States," he meticulously listed the things he had done in service to the nation, detailing what they had cost over his salary. Mr. Monroe has received more pecuniary reward from the public than any other man since the existence of the nation, John Quincy Adams wrote in 1831, and is now dying, at the age of seventy-two, in wretchedness and beggary.

He was the third president to die on the Fourth of July.

Alive, the man who had framed the famous doctrine about North and South America had been all but ignored by his countrymen. Dead, he was treated with pomp and ceremony. His New York City funeral was the biggest the city had ever seen.

d. July 4, 1831 (New York, New York), at 73, of a chronic lung illness.

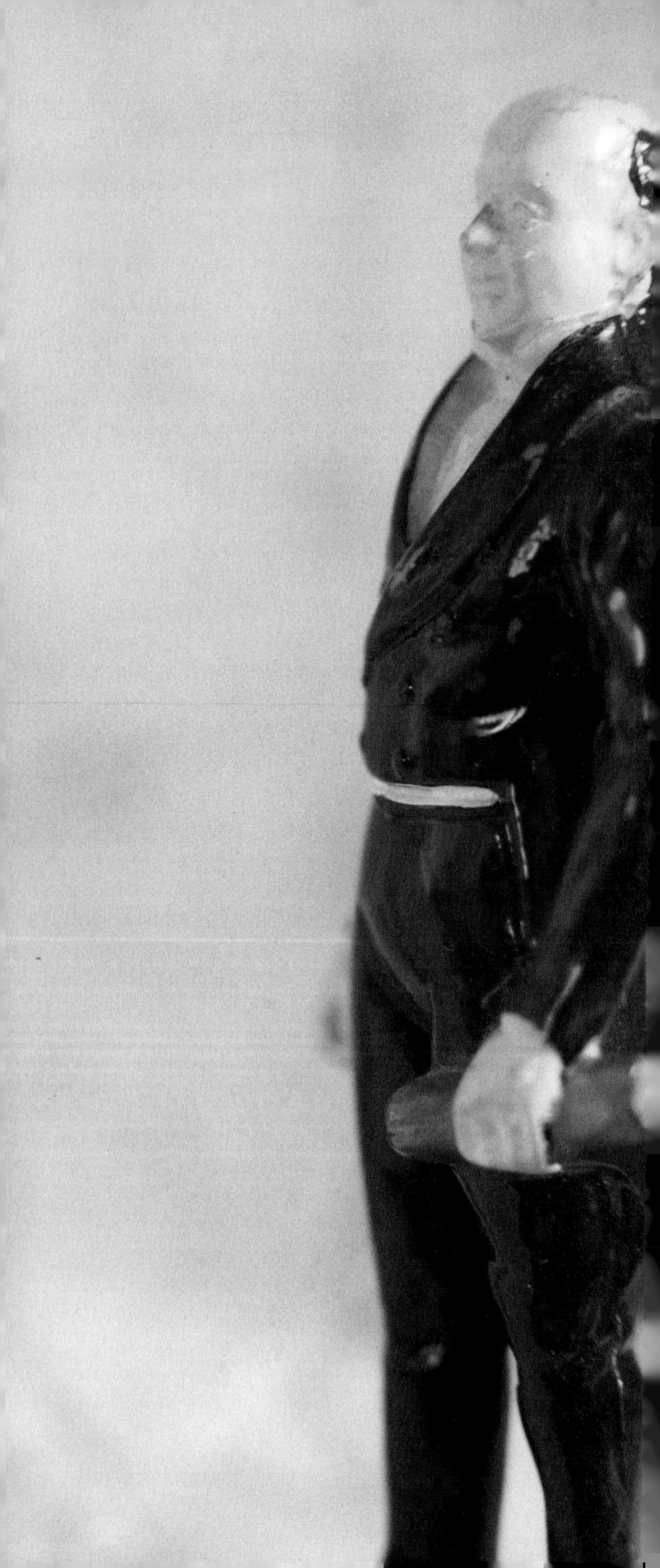

J.Q. ADAMS

6th, 1825–29

The icy-veined John Quincy Adams led a Spartan life in the White House. He rose at five, read the bible, and took a nude swim in the Potomac. To anyone walking past, the sight of the nude, pink-domed president would have been startling. One morning, the dreaded editor and journalist, Anne Royall, sat on his clothes until he agreed to answer her questions, earning her the first presidential interview ever granted to a woman.

His wife, Louisa, confided that the Adams men were peculiarly harsh and severe with their women. Few presidential relationships deteriorated as much during their White House tenure. Louisa began writing poetry and a series of bitter, sardonic plays, often skewering her husband.

J.Q. Adams served his presidential term courageously despite familial tremor, depression, stroke, and alcoholism. Watery of eye, tremulous of hand, he grew fat and flatulent.

Toilets, a novelty during his term, were given the nickname Quincy. He was the first to have such a convenience installed in the White House.

The first daguerreotype of a president was made in 1847 when J.Q. Adams was seventy-nine.

After his term, J.Q. Adams returned to public life as a congressman. While protesting the Mexican War, he suddenly collapsed on the floor of the House and was carried to a bed set up for him in the Speaker's office. In his final hours, an enterprising artist named Arthur Stansbury sketched a last portrait, the first first-hand image ever made of a dying president.

Daniel Webster overheard J.Q. Adams say, I inhabit a weak, frail, decayed tenement battered by the winds and broken in upon by the storms, and, from all I can learn, the landlord does not intend to repair!

J.Q. Adams' last words were either, *This is the last of Earth—I am composed*, or, *This is the end of Earth, but I am content.*

d. February 23, 1848 (Capitol Building, Washington, DC), at 80, from a stroke.

JACKSON

7th, 1829–37

A tall, lean, poorly educated backwoodsman with a crest of hair almost red and a temper in keeping, Andrew Jackson was a reckless horseman, cock fighter, and duelist. He was 6-feet tall and never weighed over 145 pounds. To some he seemed savage, to others heroic, earthy, masculine.

Jackson had a habit of slobbering, which he was unable to control until almost grown. A jest at this circumstance spelled combat. He pronounced development as devil-ope-ment and sublime as soo-blime.

During the 1829 presidential campaign, his wife, Rachel, was called an adulteress. The slander exposed her as a bigamist and revealed the divorce papers from her previous marriage had never been filed. Distressed by the public scandal, she took to her bed and died. Next to his heart, Jackson wore an ivory miniature depicting Rachel when she was fifty-two.

At sixty-two, grief stricken and weary, Andrew Jackson was probably the saddest man who ever entered the White House.

In the name of national security, Jackson signed into law the Indian Removal Act of 1830 and more than 45,000 American Indians were relocated to the West on a Trail of Tears. Ironically, he rescued a ten-month-old Indian boy after the Creek War, raised him as his own son, and grieved deeply when the boy died at age sixteen.

Jackson was called the son of a prostitute and a mulatto. He was also called a Jackass. He liked the name and used it for a while; later it became the symbol of the Democratic Party.

Jackson was racked by tuberculosis most of the time he was president and treated it by bleeding himself. Hard of hearing, nearly blind in one eye, his face and body swelling with painful dropsy, he spent his last days in a cushioned chair. *I am a blubber of water,* he said. His flesh from the waist down had to be literally wrapped to his body to keep it from falling away.

He was the first president born in a log cabin and the first to travel by train. America's first equestrian monument, a bronze statue depicting Jackson seated on a rearing horse, was created by sculptor Clark Mills, and stands in Lafayette Park, across from the White House.

Poll, Jackson's parrot who could speak in Spanish and English, reportedly had to be removed from Jackson's funeral because the bird was cursing in both languages.

d. June 8, 1845 (the Hermitage near Nashville, Tennessee), at 78, of chronic tuberculosis, dropsy, and heart failure.

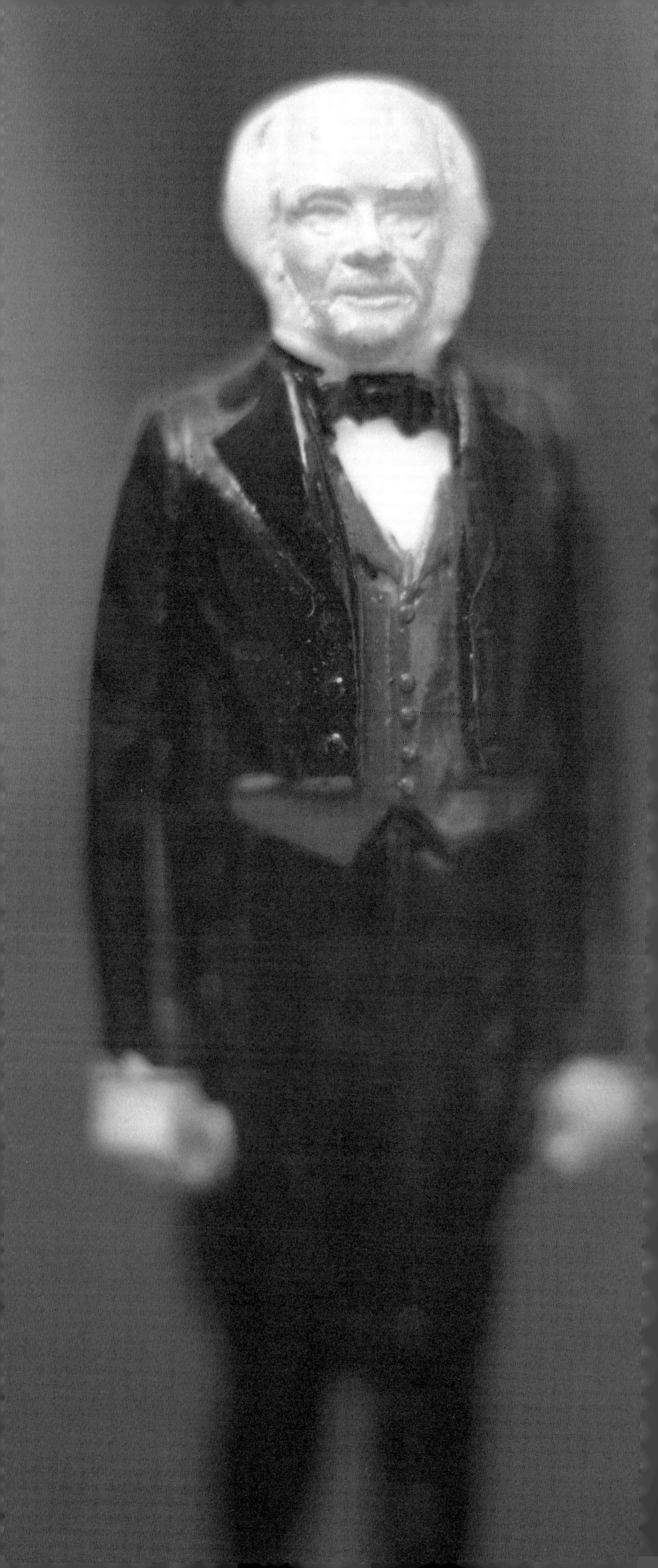

VAN BUREN

8th, 1837–41

Martin Van Buren's soldierly posture, immaculate grooming, and bright red hair made him appear taller than his 5 feet 6 inches. He was trim and slender until age sixty. In 1840, Congressman Charles Ogle of Pennsylvania maintained that the portly Van Buren had gained weight at public expense by routinely eating off gold plate in the executive mansion. He wore a corset to maintain an illusion of slimness. So skilled was he in political manipulation that he earned the nickname, The Little Magician.

Van Buren made no secret of his life's ambition. He wanted to become president, calling that office the glittering prize and my most earnest desire.

He was the first of only five presidents not of British descent. He is also the only president for whom English was not his first language. He grew up speaking Dutch.

At twenty-four he eloped to marry his childhood sweetheart and maternal cousin, Hannah Hoes. Van Buren omitted all mention and even her name from his 800-page autobiography.

An 1828 description reads: Mr. Van Buren was rather an exquisite in appearance. His complexion was a bright blond, and he dressed accordingly. His cravat was orange with modest lace tips; his vest was of a pearl hue; his trousers were white duck; his shoes were morocco; his neatly fitting gloves were yellow kid.

When Van Buren was president, the city of Washington had a population of about forty thousand. Pigs and chickens roamed the streets at will; slaves were sold openly; the terrain was swampy, malaria-ridden and crisscrossed by cow paths and open sewers. Elegant Van Buren rolled around Washington in a magnificent olive-green coach with silver-mounted harness and liveried footmen.

Blue Whiskey Van, named so because of his heavy drinking, became comatose on July 21 and died three days later.

d. July 24, 1862 (Kinderhook, New York), at 79, of asthma.

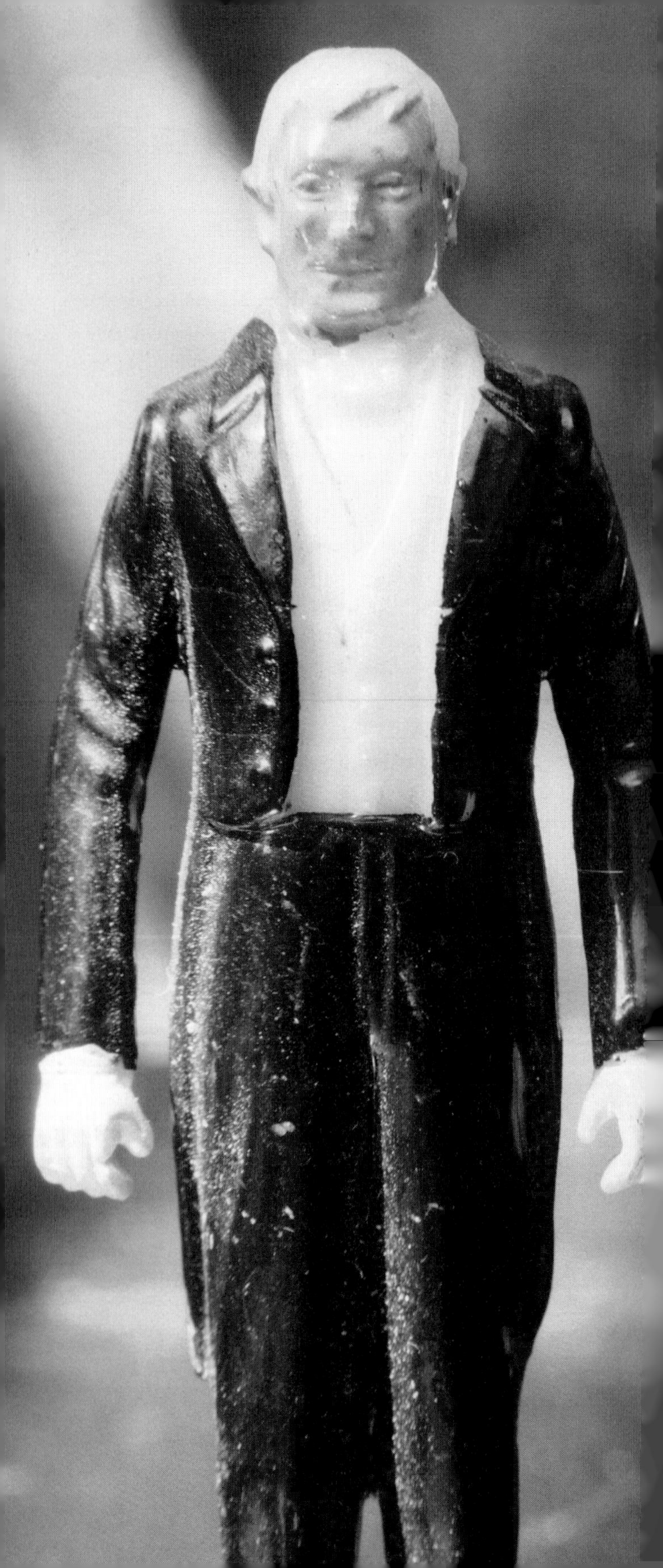

W.H. HARRISON

9th, 1841

William Henry Harrison was stern, tall, and austere. He ate only cheese and milk products. He was completely honest and happily married to Anna, who bore him ten children.

A notice in the papers announced W.H. Harrison would shake no hands at his inauguration. I cannot bear this, don't trouble me, he said, his arm sore and his hand swollen from campaigning. He delivered a forty-minute inauguration speech (written by Daniel Webster) in the rain with no overcoat.

When W.H. Harrison took office in 1841 at the age of sixty-eight, he was the oldest man to become president—a record that stood for 140 years until Ronald Reagan became president at the age of sixty-nine. He was also the first to die in office. His term, the shortest in the history of the presidency, lasted 30 days, 11 hours, and 30 minutes.

Most of W.H. Harrison's business, during his month-long presidency, involved receiving office seekers. He would promise anything to a friend, and if sincerity alone could keep promises, he would never have reneged on one. But he was overdrawing his account, overpromising his partisans, and overfeeding his friends.

Harrison helped bring down Shawnee warrior Tecumseh in the Battle of Tippecanoe in 1811. In retaliation, Tecumseh's brother, the Prophet Tenskwatawa, is said to have cursed the US Presidency, so that those elected every 20 years would die in office. That's Harrison, 1840; Lincoln, 1860; Garfield, 1880; McKinley, 1900; Harding, 1920; Roosevelt, 1940; Kennedy, 1960; and Reagan, 1980. The Prophet said, And when each one dies, let everyone remember the death of my people.

Speaking to John Tyler, W.H. Harrison's last words were: *Sir, I wish you to understand the true principles of the government. I wish them carried out. I ask nothing more.*

d. April 4, 1841 (Washington, DC), at 68, of pneumonia.

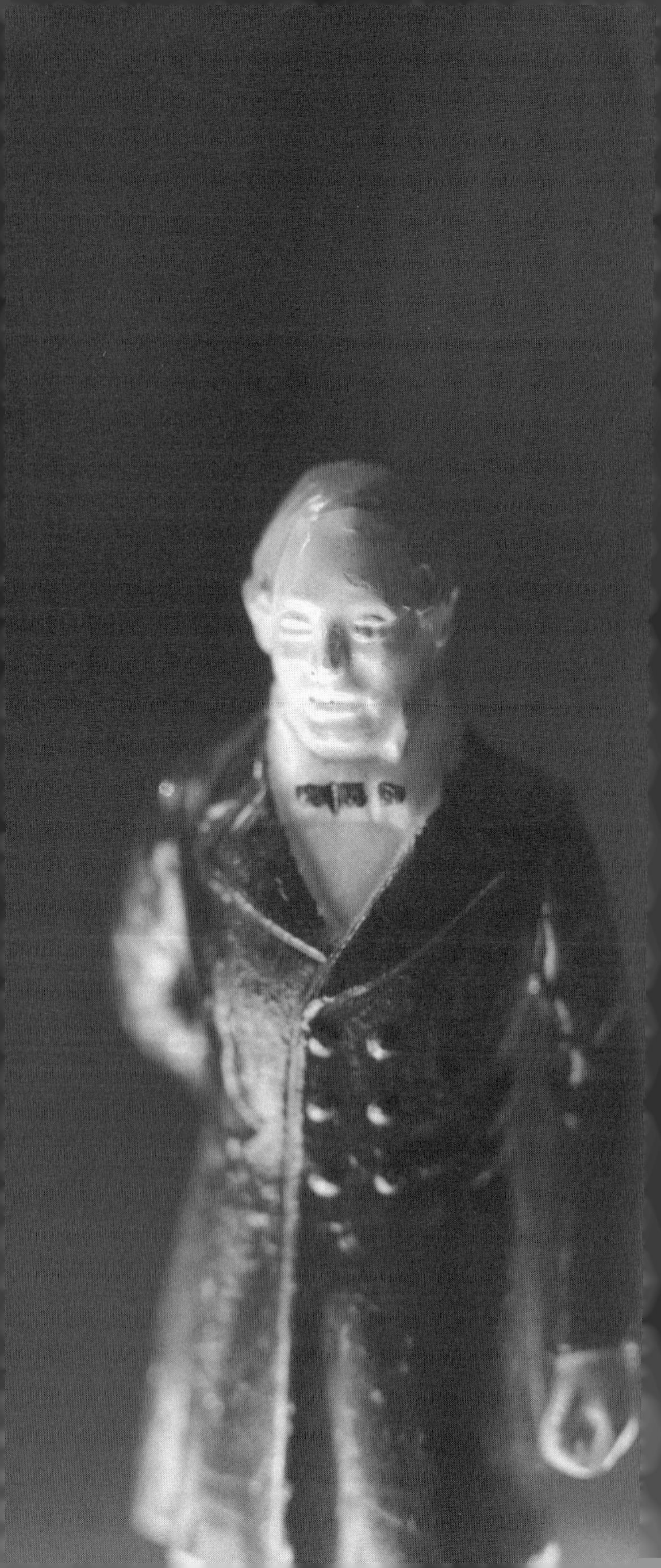

TYLER

10th, 1841-45

Honest John Tyler, a tall, thin man with a high-bridged nose and blue eyes, was kindly and of less-than-mediocre ability. His presidency was rarely taken seriously in his time; opponents called him His Accidency.

Tyler was the first vice president to reach the White House through the death of a president. When he got the news, he was on his knees, shooting marbles with his children.

His first wife, Letitia, who mothered seven of his fifteen children, was an invalid and died in 1842. Priscilla Cooper Tyler, daughter-in-law of the president and a professional actress, assumed the position of White House hostess. Tyler did not endear himself to the country when, two years after Letitia's death, at the age of fifty-four, he married Julia Gardiner, who was thirty years younger and whose father had been his friend. Her portrait was the first of a president's wife to be hung in the White House. Tyler is the only president to have had three different First Ladies during his time in office.

Tyler had several illegitimate children. His son John Dunjee was born a slave and became a prominent minister.

Tyler's favorite horse is buried at his Sherwood Forest Plantation with a gravestone that reads, Here lies the body of my good horse The General. For twenty years he bore me around the circuit of my practice and in all that time he never made me blunder. Would that his master could say the same.

When Tyler was president, Samuel Morse sent the first telegraphic message: What hath God wrought?

Tyler's final words were: *Perhaps it is best.*

d. January 18, 1862 (Richmond, Virginia), at 71, of biliousness.

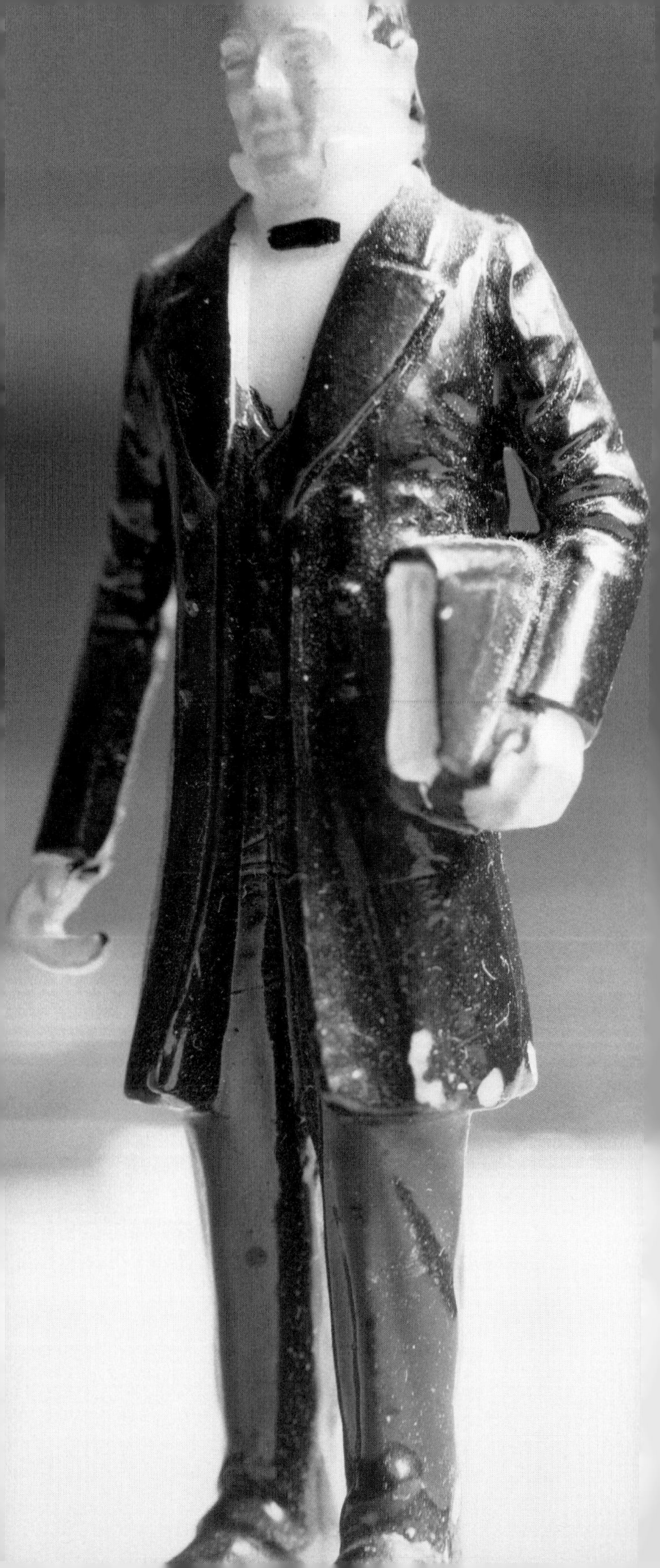

POLK

11th, 1845–49

Somber, stern, thin-lipped, James Knox Polk was physically undistinguishable.

The least conspicuous man who had ever been nominated for president, Polk called himself the hardest-working man in this country. His wife, Sarah Childress, lightened his workload by becoming his competent confidential secretary.

A gallstone operation, without anesthesia or antiseptics, may have left him sterile.

Polk explained his handshaking technique in his diary: A man should shake and not be shaken, grip and not be gripped, taking care always to squeeze the hand of his adversary as hard as he squeezed him. When I observed a strong man approaching I generally took advantage of him by being a little quicker than he was and seizing him by the tips of his fingers, giving him a hearty shake, and thus preventing him from getting a full grip upon me.

The most blatant of our expansionist presidents, Polk sent his message to Congress declaring war on Mexico. General Winfield Scott took possession of Mexico City on September 14, 1847. The halls of Montezuma were invaded. Subsequently, Polk suffered from chronic diarrhea, succumbing to it three months out of office.

Polk's last words were: *I love you, Sarah. For all eternity, I love you.* Polk left most of his estate to his wife, with the request that she free their slaves upon her death.

d. June 15, 1849 (Nashville, Tennessee), at 53, of chronic diarrhea.

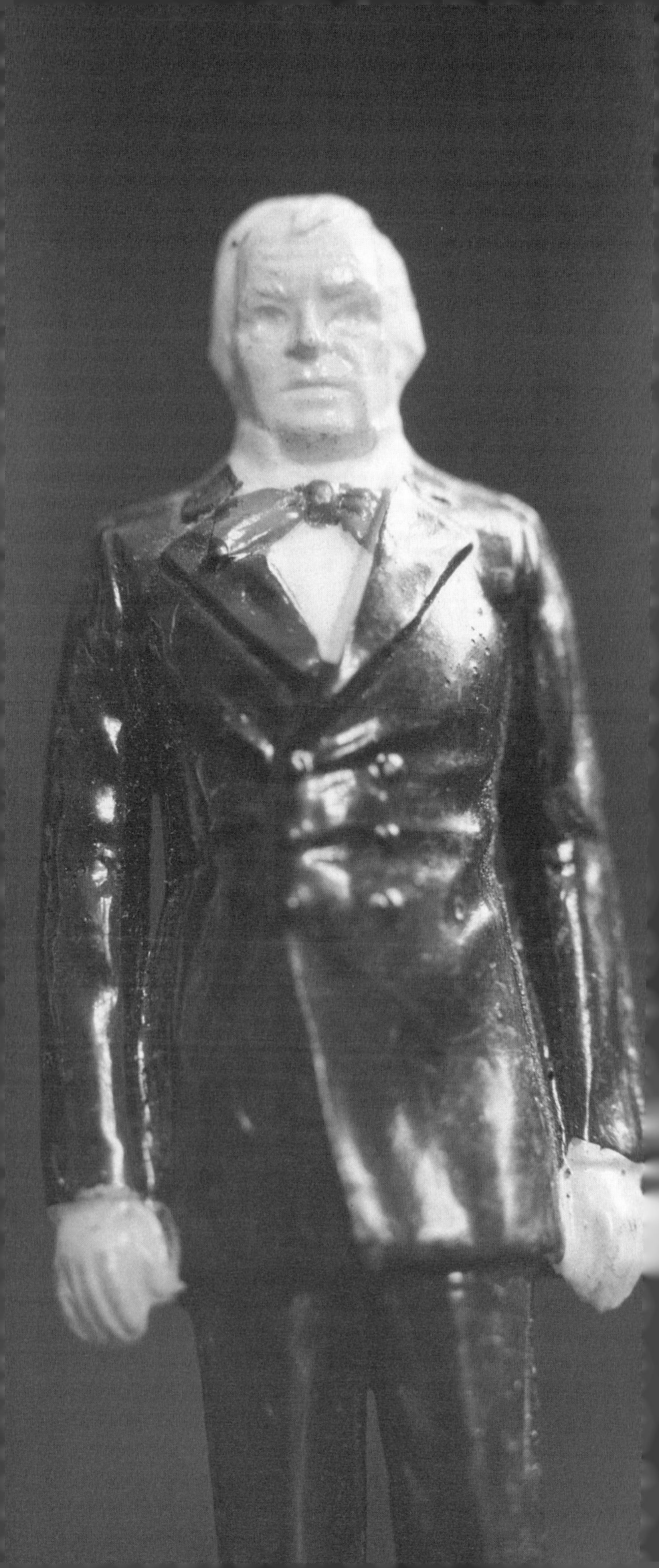

TAYLOR

12th, 1849–50

Short, dumpy, and thick-necked, Zachary Taylor had a head big enough to rest on the body of a giant. His legs were so short he required the help of an orderly to lift him into the saddle when he mounted his warhorse.

He had little schooling, no knowledge of law, government, or politics, and had never cast a vote in his life. He was nominated without anyone knowing where he stood on any issue.

He was the first Regular Army man to become president. In or out of uniform, Old Rough and Ready was no stickler for spit and polish, and his appearance was frayed, dusty, and wrinkled. His near-sightedness caused him to squint, and he kept one eye closed while reading to prevent double vision. This brought his heavy brows down and gave the impression of a fierce scowl.

Taylor was the second cousin of James Madison.

He chewed tobacco and spit it accurately. He had a stutter.

His wife, Margaret Smith, smoked a corncob pipe in the privacy of her rooms, never appeared at White House functions, and outlived him by two years.

Although some suspect that Taylor was poisoned in the end, it is more likely that he contracted Typhoid fever from cherries he ate on the Fourth of July. His last words were, *I regret nothing, but I am sorry that I am about to leave my friends.*

d. July 9, 1850 (in the White House), at 65, worn out by war and politics.

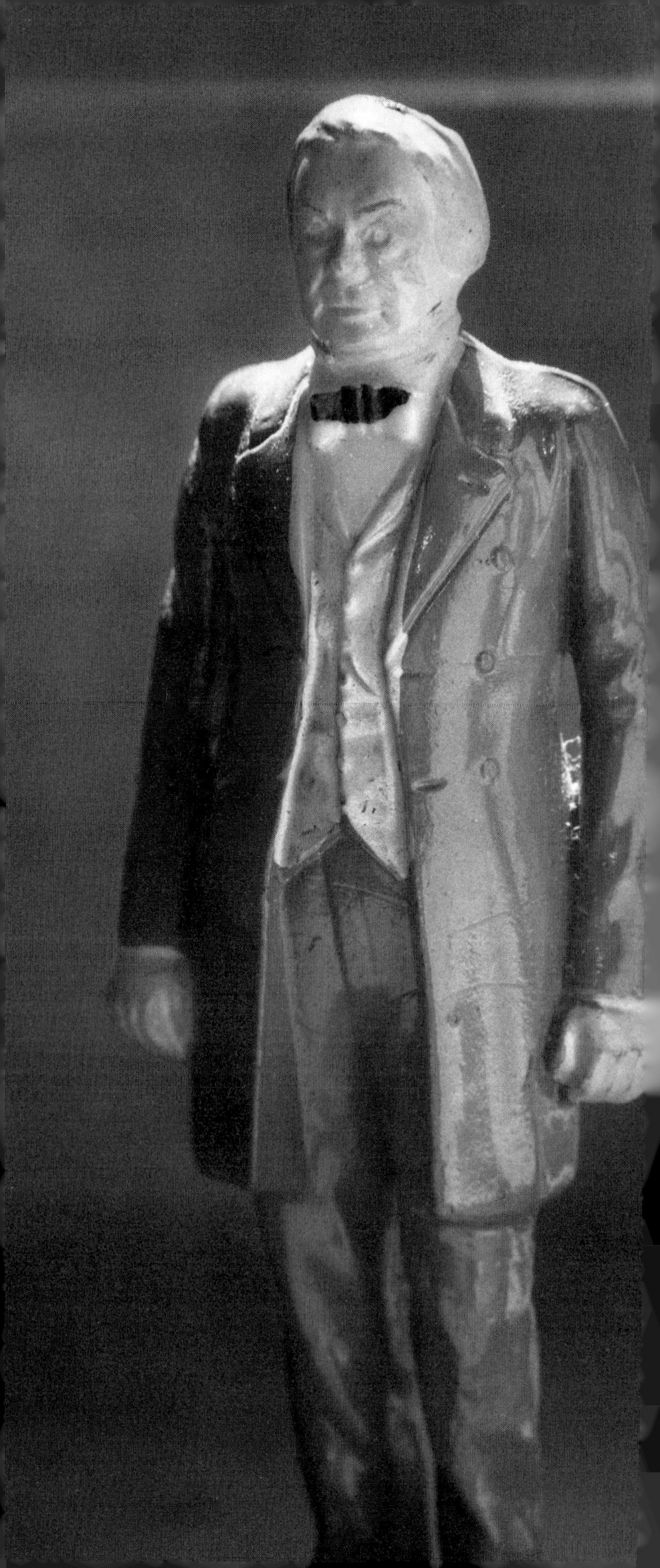

FILLMORE

13th, 1850–53

Millard Fillmore was the second president born in a log cabin.

An impressive figure, Fillmore stood 6-feet tall and handsome. He enjoyed dressing in the latest fashions, displaying impeccable good taste that masked his humble origins. His voice was deep and masculine, but he spoke softly and carefully.

He was seventeen before he saw a dictionary. He was illiterate until adulthood.

In 1826, he married Abigail Powers, a schoolteacher, who helped him with his education. In the years of their marriage, they collected over 4,000 books. It was to the credit of Abigail that a library and, disputably, a bathtub were installed in the White House.

Fillmore suffered from an eye disorder that limited his ability to read by candlelight.

He is the only president to have had his first military experience after his presidency. He helped organize the Union Continentals, a militia unit composed of older men, in which he eventually rose to major.

He did not smoke or drink and was fastidious about his health.

His last words, upon being fed some soup: *The nourishment is palatable.*

d. March 8, 1874 (Buffalo, New York), at 74, of a stroke.

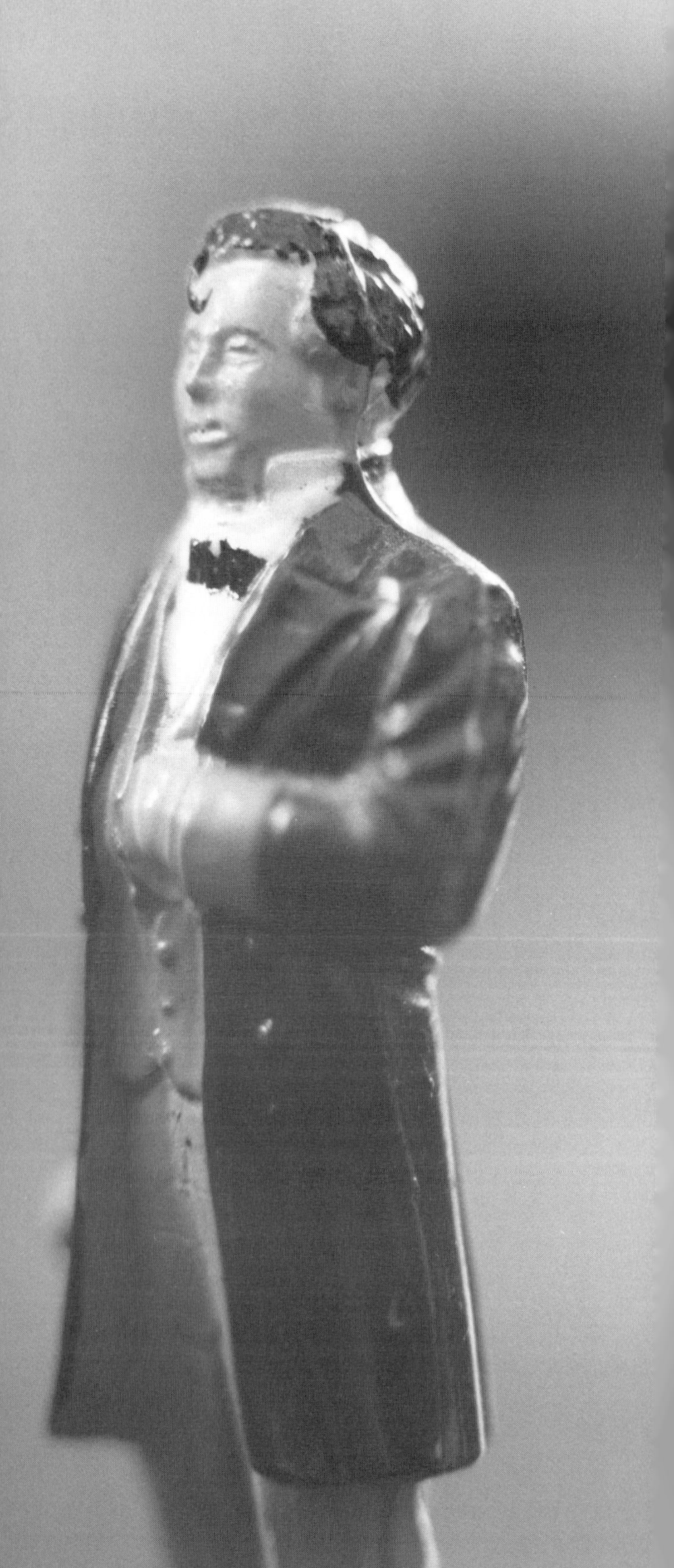

PIERCE

14th, 1853–57

Franklin Pierce was the most unambitious man ever to run for office.

He is the great-great granduncle of George W. Bush.

Handsome Frank Pierce probably had more personal friends than any other president.

In 1852, Nathaniel Hawthorne wrote Pierce's autobiography. He described Pierce as, with the boy and man in him, vivacious, mirthful, slender, of a fair complexion, with light hair that had a curl in it. His bright and cheerful aspect made a kind of sunshine.

Hawthorne spoke in awed tones of Pierce's good luck, but the president was anything but lucky. As brigadier general, in Winfield Scott's drive on Mexico City, Pierce's horse bucked and tossed him forward so that the pommel of his saddle was driven into his groin. He fainted. Called a coward, Pierce was unable to find heroic redemption.

Two months before his inauguration, Pierce and his wife, Jane Means Appleton, were in a train that derailed and toppled over an embankment. They sustained slight physical injuries, but their son was practically decapitated in front of their eyes. He was their third son to die. Jane decided that God had taken their son so her husband would have no family distractions while president.

He was the first president to commit his inaugural speech to memory.

In 1853, while in office, Pierce was arrested for running over an old woman with his horse. The case was dropped due to insufficient evidence.

He was the first president to have a Christmas tree in the White House.

He was an alcoholic. At the end of his term, when asked what a president should do after leaving office, he sighed: *There's nothing left... but to get drunk.*

d. October 8, 1869 (Concord, New Hampshire), at 64, from cirrhosis of the liver.

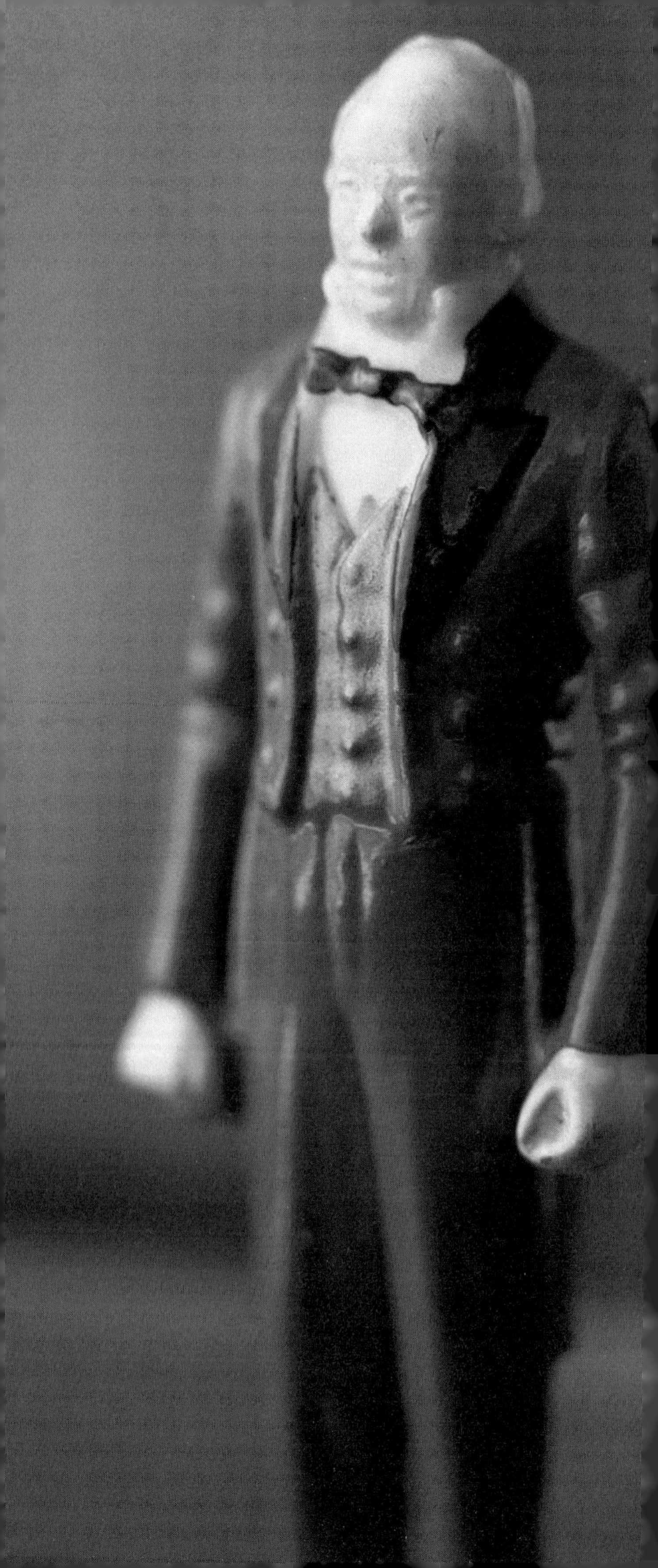

BUCHANAN

15th, 1857–61

Due to an eye defect, James Buchanan had the peculiarity of carrying his head slightly forward and sideways, like a poll parrot, giving the impression of exceptional courtesy and sensitivity to others. His enemies said it was due to his having tried to hang himself years earlier.

At the time of Buchanan's inauguration, in the city of Washington, people emptied slops and refuse in the gutters, threw dead domestic animals in the canal, and trundled the carts of night soil out to the commons, ten blocks north of the White House.

Buchanan was a gentle, diplomatic person, religiously fatalistic in his approach to life. He stood 6-feet tall and was a heavy man. President Polk said, Buchanan sometimes acts like an old maid.

Buchanan enjoyed a twenty-year intimate friendship with Senator William Rufus de Vane King. He referred to King as Aunt Nancy. They shared quarters in Washington, DC for sixteen years. When King died in 1853, Buchanan wrote, I am now solitary and alone, having no companion in the house with me. I have gone a wooing to several gentlemen, but have not succeeded with any one of them.

Buchanan was the only bachelor president and the last to wear a stock.

In 1866, Buchanan published the first presidential memoir.

On the day before his death, he said: *History will vindicate my memory.*

d. June 1, 1868 (Lancaster, Pennsylvania), at 77, of respiratory failure.

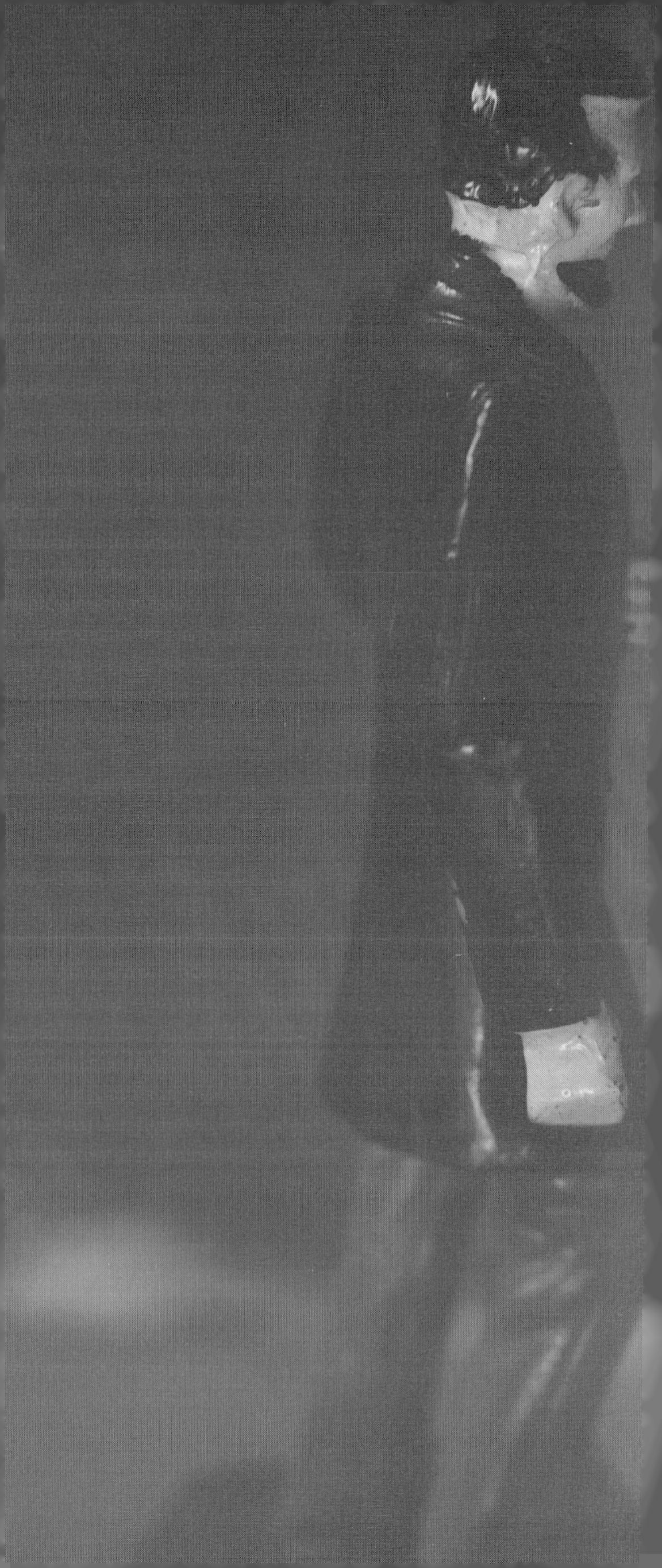

LINCOLN

16th, 1861–65

Abraham Lincoln described himself in a letter: If any personal description of me is thought desirable, it may be said I am, in height, six feet four inches, nearly; lean in flesh, weighing on an average of one hundred and eighty pounds; dark complexion, with coarse black hair and grey eyes. No other marks or brands recollected.

Lincoln was of Melungeon descent. Cartoonists nicknamed him, Abraham Africanus the First. Walt Whitman wrote, I see very plainly Abraham Lincoln's dark brown face, with the deep cut lines, the eyes always to me, with a deep latent sadness in the expression. None of the artists or pictures have caught the deep though subtle and indirect expression of this man's face.

William G. Greene told Billy Herndon, Speaking of Lincoln physical Strength let me say I saw him lift one thousand & twenty four pounds.

Lincoln fought clinical depression all his life. Lincoln went Crazy, his closest friend Joshua Speed recalled, — had to remove razors from his room—take away all Knives and other such dangerous things—&—it was terrible. For four years the two men shared a bed, along with their most private fears and desires. Their births, the loins and tissues of their fathers and mothers, accident, fate, providence, wrote Carl Sandburg in 1926, had given these two men streaks of lavender, spots soft as May violets.

Lincoln's marriage to Mary Todd was indisputably rocky. They fought hard and bitterly, often and audibly. Adjudged insane in 1875, she was, however, later found to be competent, though she suffered from arthritis, migraine headaches, diabetes, and female troubles.

Lincoln had a penetrating and far-reaching voice that could be heard over great distances. He was not a good sleeper, and he liked cats and kittens as he did no other animal.

Lincoln caught syphilis from a prostitute in 1832.

Mary Todd admonished him not to hold her hand at Ford's Theater during the performance of *Our American*

Cousin because people might see them. Lincoln said, It doesn't really matter. He was laughing when he was shot.

The last breath was drawn at 21 minutes and 55 seconds past 7 A.M. and the last heartbeat flickered at 22 minutes and 10 seconds past the hour on Saturday, April 15, 1865. Over the worn features had come, wrote John Hay, a look of unspeakable peace.

Leo Tolstoy said, Of all the great national heroes and statesmen of history Lincoln is the only real giant. He was a Christ in miniature.

d. April 15, 1865 (Washington, DC), at 56, felled by a .44 caliber Derringer Pistol.

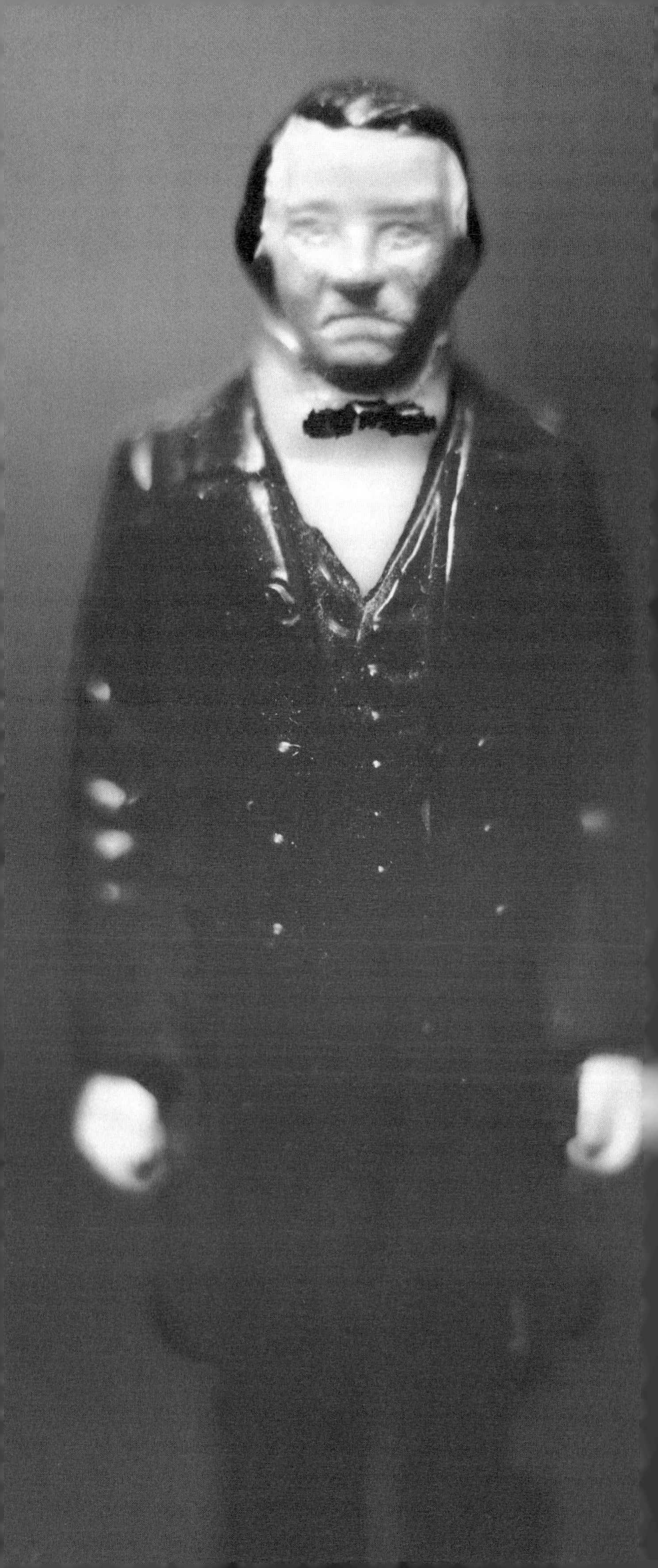

JOHNSON

17th, 1865–69

Sturdily built, of medium height, Andrew Johnson had black hair and piercing eyes set in a face that Charles Dickens called remarkable. He was known as The Grim Presence.

The only president who never spent a single day in a schoolroom, he was a poor white of lowly parentage, born in a shack. He dressed simply, always in black.

Johnson did not master the basics of reading, grammar, or math until he met his wife, Eliza, at the age of seventeen. Determined that her husband should amount to something, Eliza hired a man to read to him as he worked, and she taught him writing and arithmetic at night. She was also a soothing, calming influence on his easily ruffled feathers. He had a deep inner sense of insecurity, and Eliza had a soft voice that could reach him in his darkest moments.

In his lifetime Johnson was city councilman, mayor, state representative, state senator, governor, representative, senator, vice president, and president. He is the only person to have held all of the non-judicial positions in the American political system. He also possessed, in the words of a fellow Tennessean who knew him well, a deep-seated, burning hatred of all men who stood in his way.

Undoubtedly the greatest misfortune that ever befell Johnson was the assassination of president Lincoln. The student of history is forced to conclude that his posthumous fame would have been brighter without the high honor of being promoted to president and the consequences it entailed.

On February 24, 1868, Johnson became the first president to be impeached.

The unpopular Johnson was virtually ignored by the press when he died. But his New York Times obituary stated, The Boy Who Never Went To School Grows Up To Be President. The history this man leaves is a rare one. His career was remarkable, even in this country; it would have been quite impossible in any other.

d. July 31, 1875 (in Greeneville, Tennessee), at 66, of a stroke.

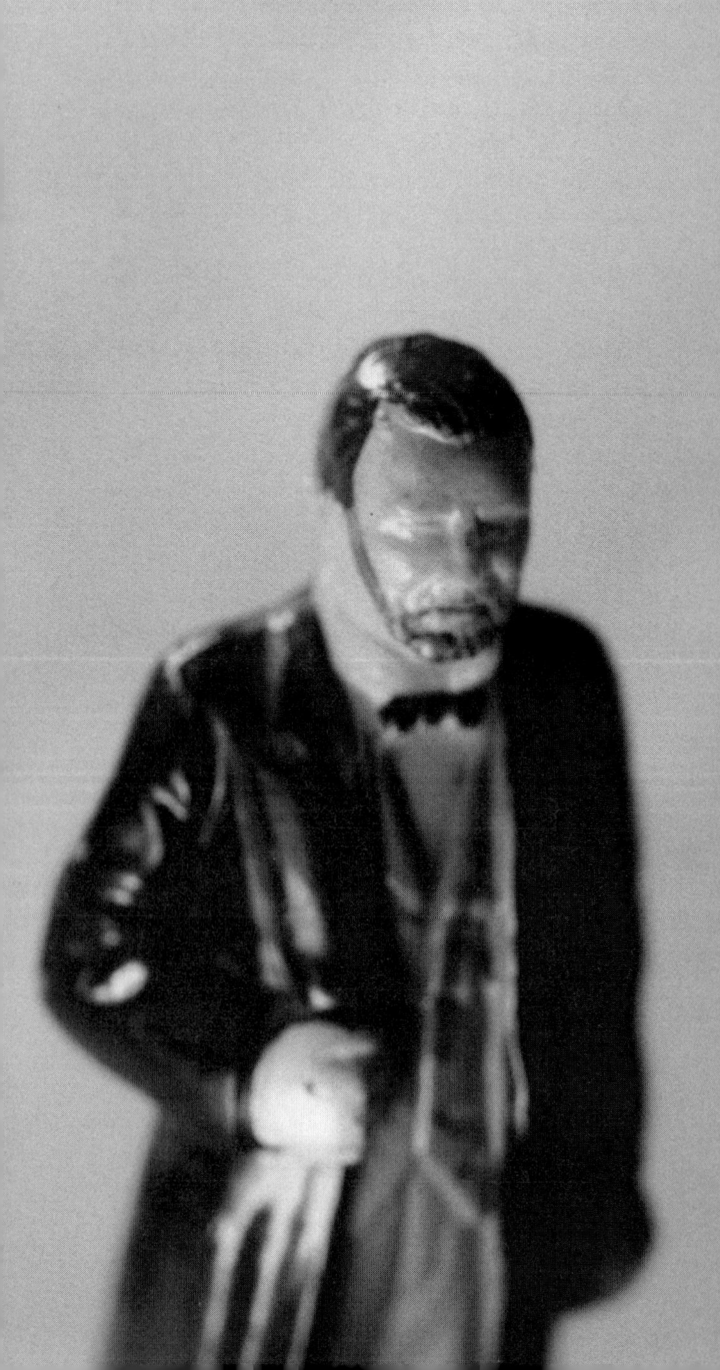

GRANT

18th, 1869–77

Hiram Ulysses Grant had unusually small hands and feet. His physical modesty was extreme. He said that no one had seen him naked since he was a small boy.

His middle name was "Ulysses" and he admitted that the "S" in his name stood for nothing. Grant said, My family is American, and has been for generations, in all its branches, direct and collateral. Through the Delano family, Grant was a fourth cousin once removed to Franklin Roosevelt and a sixth cousin once removed of Grover Cleveland.

Julia Dent Grant was by no means a beauty. As First Lady, she considered an operation to correct an eye defect, but the president liked her, he said, with her eyes crossed and would not have her different.

Lacking drive or decision in civilian life, he was a failure in everything he did. But in war he was a lion.

After his term in office, Grant followed his son into the firm Grant & Ward as a silent partner. On May 5, 1884, when brokers learned of the $16 million failure of the firm, panic swept Wall Street. In 1909, after ten years at Sing Sing, Ferdinand Ward told the *New York Herald,* It was believed I might reveal something which would show General Grant's connection with the failure of our firm. I would not have done this if I could. I could not if I would. General Grant was always so much the child in business matters that it would have been impossible for him had he been so minded to hasten much by any overt act the fall of our house.

After the crash, Grant's personal assets amounted to less than $200.

He was an acute alcoholic.

Penniless, in disgrace, and dying of cancer of the throat, the old General began to write. Grant finished the two-volume work on July 19, 1885; he died five days later. With Mark Twain as publisher, the *Personal Memoirs of U.S. Grant* quickly became a best seller, and the Grants, who received seventy-five percent of the royalties, made

$450,000 from the book. Grant thus re-established the family fortune and made the last years for his beloved goose of a wife comfortable and happy.

Grant wrote: A verb is anything that signifies to be; to do; or to suffer. I signify all three. His last word was: *Water*.

d. July 23, 1885 (New York, New York), at 63, of carcinoma of the tongue and tonsils.

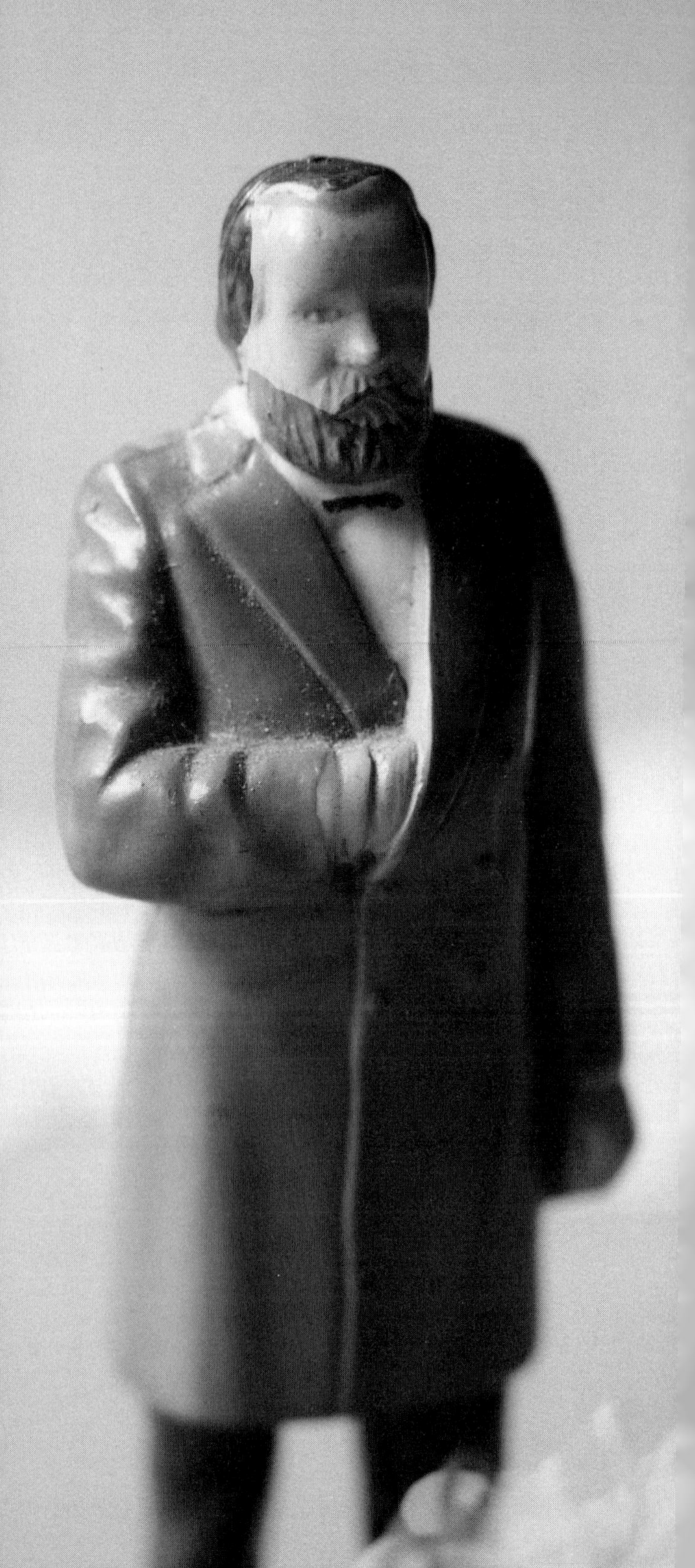

HAYES

19th, 1877–81

Rutherford Birchard Hayes was one of the most mediocre-looking men ever to run for president. He was short, rumpled in dress, and wore a rat's-nest beard. He had no charisma. Henry Adams described Hayes as a third-rate nonentity, whose only recommendation is that he is obnoxious to no one.

His delicate health kept him from school in his early childhood, and he was as timid and nervous as a girl, with an aversion to the rough and mischievous ways of schoolboys. A journal entry states: Welladay, more faults to cure... Trifling remarks, boyish conduct, etc., are among my crying sins. Mend, mend!

Hayes and his sister, Fanny, had affection for each other that spilled over the customary bounds of sibling devotion. He wrote in a letter to Fanny, in 1840: The only news here now is, the big monkey is dead and pussy has got the hydr– I forget the rest of the word. Even after Fanny's marriage, she wrote him constantly, begging him to visit her and assuring him that he was daily the object of my waking thoughts & utmost nightly of my dreams. When Fanny died in 1856 in childbirth, Hayes wrote to a friend, Oh, what a blow it is! During all my life she has been the dear one! Hayes wrote to his wife: You are Sister Fanny to me now.

His wife, Lucy, was the first college graduate to serve as First Lady.

Hayes was the first president to have a telephone or typewriter in the White House.

Hayes is also reputed to be the first president to have had his voice recorded, by Thomas Edison in 1877 with his newly invented phonograph, but the recording is lost, and this fact cannot be verified. His last words were: *I know that I am going where Lucy is.*

d. January 17, 1893 (Fremont, Ohio), at 70, of a heart attack.

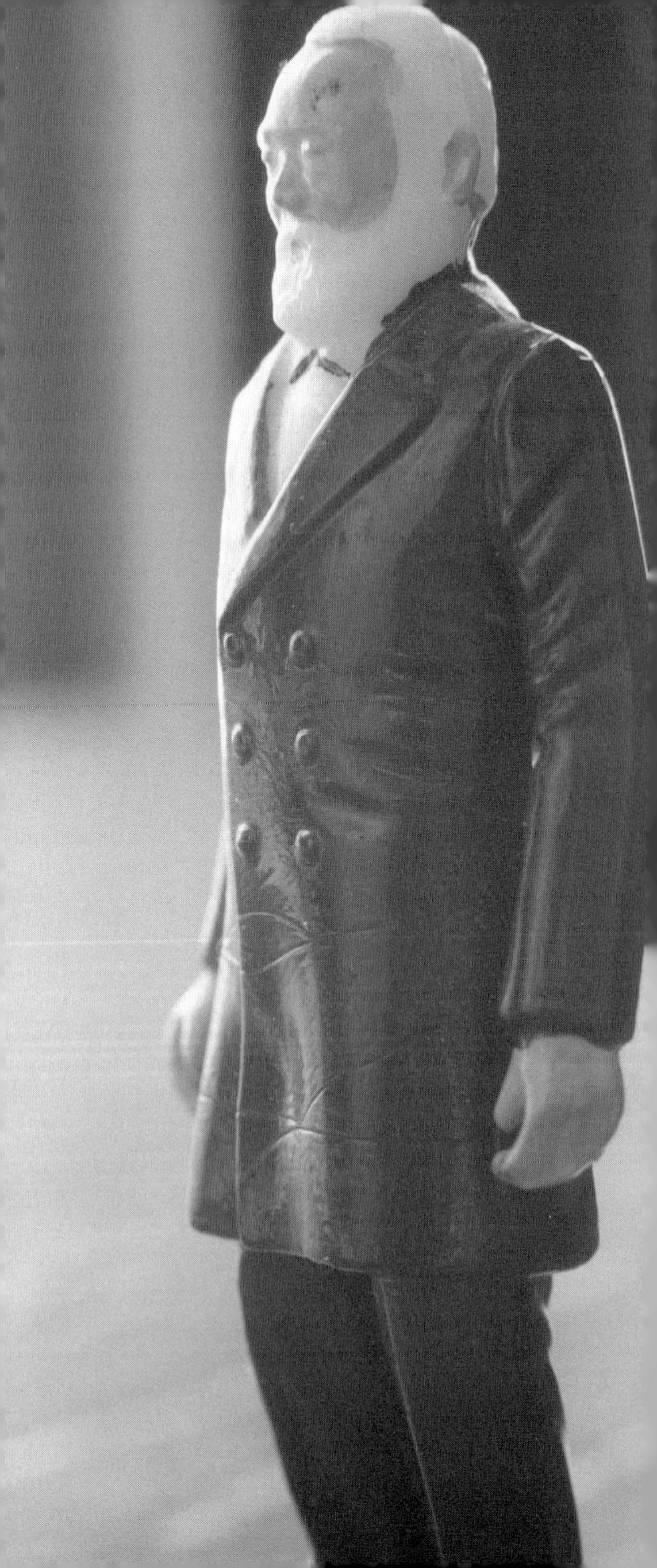

GARFIELD

20th, 1881

James Abram Garfield was strong, broad shouldered, and substantial, with a large head and bushy, light-brown hair. His features were plain but manly and sensible. Garfield was elected president at age forty-nine. He was 6-feet tall and weighed 185 pounds.

He was one of the few scholarly men of the presidency. A lover of poetry and the classics, he wrote passable verse, could read and write in Latin and Greek, and used to entertain his friends by simultaneously writing Latin with one hand and Greek with the other.

At rest he may have seemed ordinary, but when engaged in public speaking, a contemporary noted that Garfield's voice took on a sort of explosive quality as he moved toward his climax, his language gained the height of simple and massive eloquence, and his arguments came forth like a solid shot from a cannon.

Charles J. Guiteau borrowed ten dollars and purchased a .44 caliber British Bulldog pistol. According to Garfield biographer Allan Peskin, Guiteau chose the particular model because he believed it would look more imposing in the museum case that it was destined to occupy. On July 2, 1881, Guiteau fired two bullets into Garfield. One caused a superficial arm wound. The whereabouts of the second bullet was a mystery despite even the efforts of Alexander Graham Bell, who used his newly invented induction balance, better known now as a metal detector, to locate the bullet.

By the time Garfield died on September 19, his doctors had turned a three-inch deep harmless wound into a twenty-inch-long contaminated gash, stretching from his ribs to his groin and oozing more pus each day. Garfield's medical bill was $18,500.

For some period after the shooting, Garfield was fed rectally. It is likely that he died of malnutrition.

At his trial, Guiteau admitted shooting the president but denied killing him. Instead, he claimed that Garfield's physicians killed him. Guiteau was executed because his defense was not strong enough.

d. September 19, 1881 (Elberon, New Jersey), at 49, assassinated.

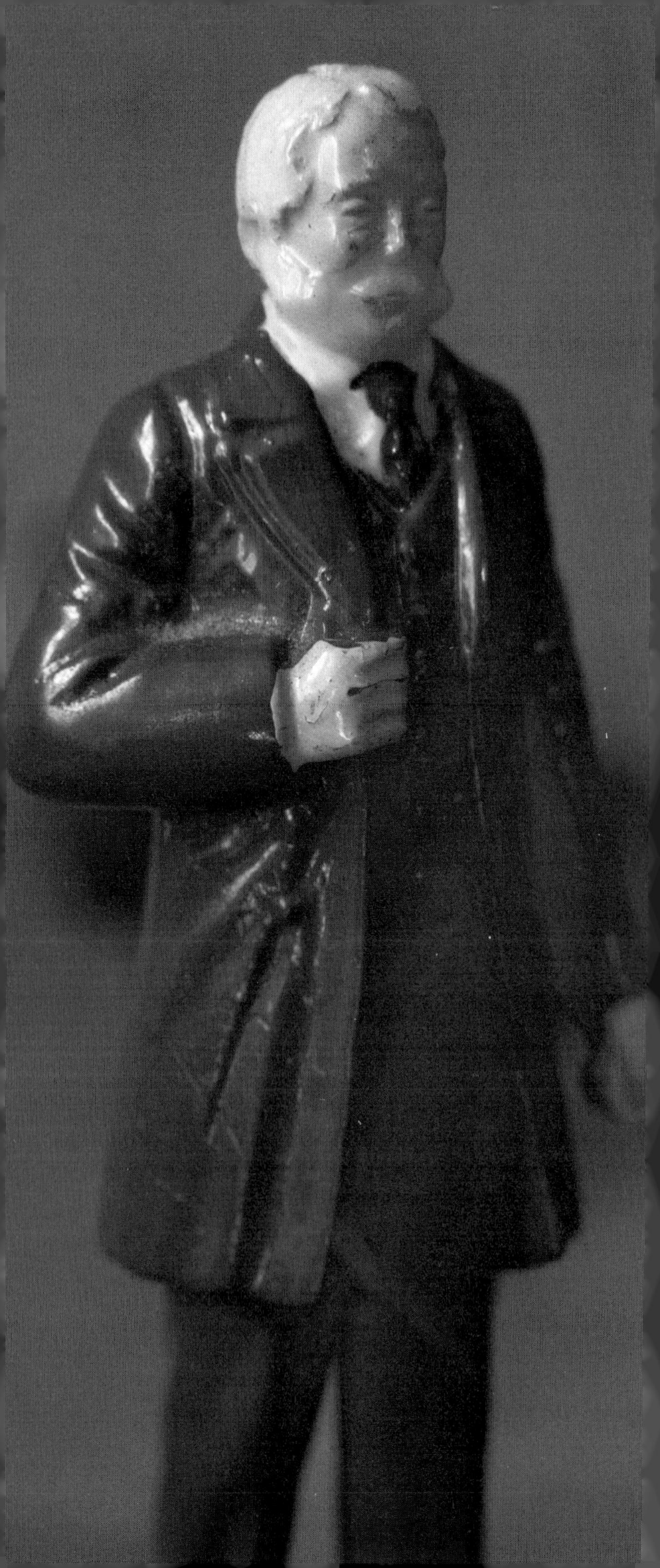

ARTHUR

21th, 1881–85

Chester Arthur, a machine politician from New York, looked like a president—he was over 6-feet tall, courtly, always stylishly dressed and trimmed to the perfection point. He did not like to dress himself but preferred to be dressed by boys. He kept eighty pairs of pants in his wardrobe and changed them several times a day.

Woodrow Wilson described him as a nonentity with side whiskers.

He spent large sums for flowers and never forgot to place a fresh bouquet before the photograph of his dead wife, Ellen Herndon. Four young women proposed to him on the day he left office.

Publisher Alexander K. McClure wrote, No man ever entered the presidency so profoundly and widely distrusted, and no one ever retired more generally respected. The one-time Collector of the Port of New York earned the moniker, The Father of Civil Service.

In 1882, various people close to the president noticed that he was becoming increasingly depressed, irritable, and lethargic. A cousin described Arthur as sick in body and soul. He was diagnosed as suffering from Bright's disease. His terminal illness was kept secret from the American people.

He told a friend: *After all, life is not worth living. I might as well give up the struggle for it now as at any other time and submit to the inevitable.* Arthur expired, exhausted by the strains of office.

d. November 18, 1886 (New York, New York), at 57, of a massive cerebral hemorrhage.

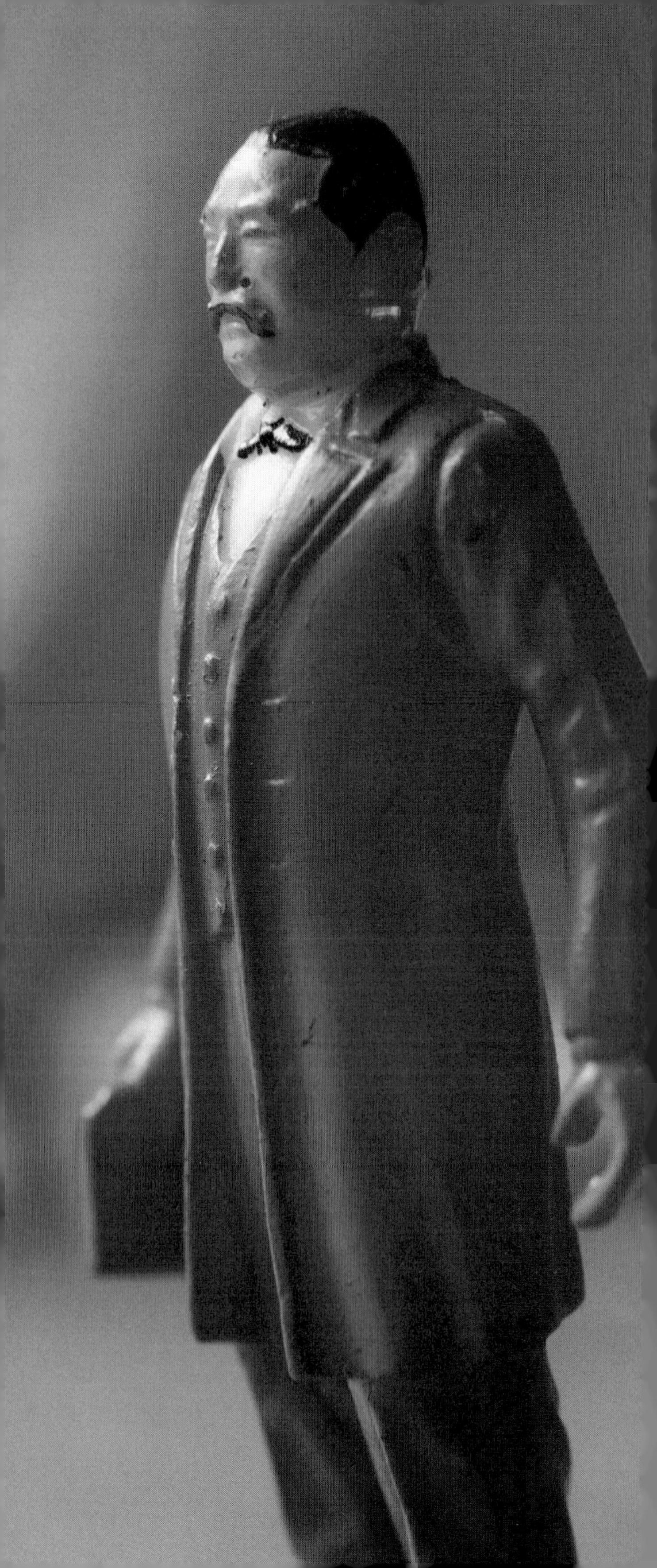

CLEVELAND

22nd & 24th, 1885–89, 93–97

Grover Cleveland was not physically attractive. He weighed 260 pounds and was bull-necked. He was the second-heaviest president after Taft.

His stubbornness earned him the title His Obstinacy.

Cleveland liked cigars and developed oral cancer. He treated it in secrecy on a friend's yacht. The hole on the roof of his mouth left by surgery was filled with a removable rubber plug. To keep it secret, Cleveland did more lying in the period just before his surgery, and the period immediately thereafter, than in the remainder of his life.

Even so, he had the reputation for being ugly-honest. Charged with seduction and bastardy, Cleveland said, It is true. Tell the truth! To the surprise and dismay of mentors and opponents alike, he remained incorruptible.

Cleveland evaded the draft by borrowing $300 to hire a man to go in his stead.

He was in a saloon drinking a glass of beer when a number of Democratic politicians looking for a candidate for mayor in a joking manner said, Let us nominate Grover. In less than four years he was inaugurated president of the United States. Cleveland did few things badly.

When considering whether to run again, in 1892, Cleveland wrote, I do not want the office. It involves a responsibility beyond human strength to a man who brings conscience to the discharge of his duties.

He taught for a while in a school for the blind in New York City.

When his law partner and closest friend was suddenly killed, thrown from a buggy, Cleveland acted as executor of the estate. He looked after the widow and her eleven-year-old daughter. No one suspected that Cleveland had more than a paternal interest in Francis Folsom, who, at twenty-one, became the youngest First Lady in the US history. Cleveland was the first president to be married in the White House.

Cleveland's final illness was discussed at a meeting: The Secretary of Commerce and Labor announced,

Cleveland is very ill, in fact he has pretty much lost his mind. The Secretary of State remarked, When a man had been exerting great mental force and then suddenly stopped, it was sure to happen. The Secretary of Agriculture added, More surely kill him.

d. June 24, 1908 (Princeton, New Jersey), at 71, possibly of Alzheimer's disease.

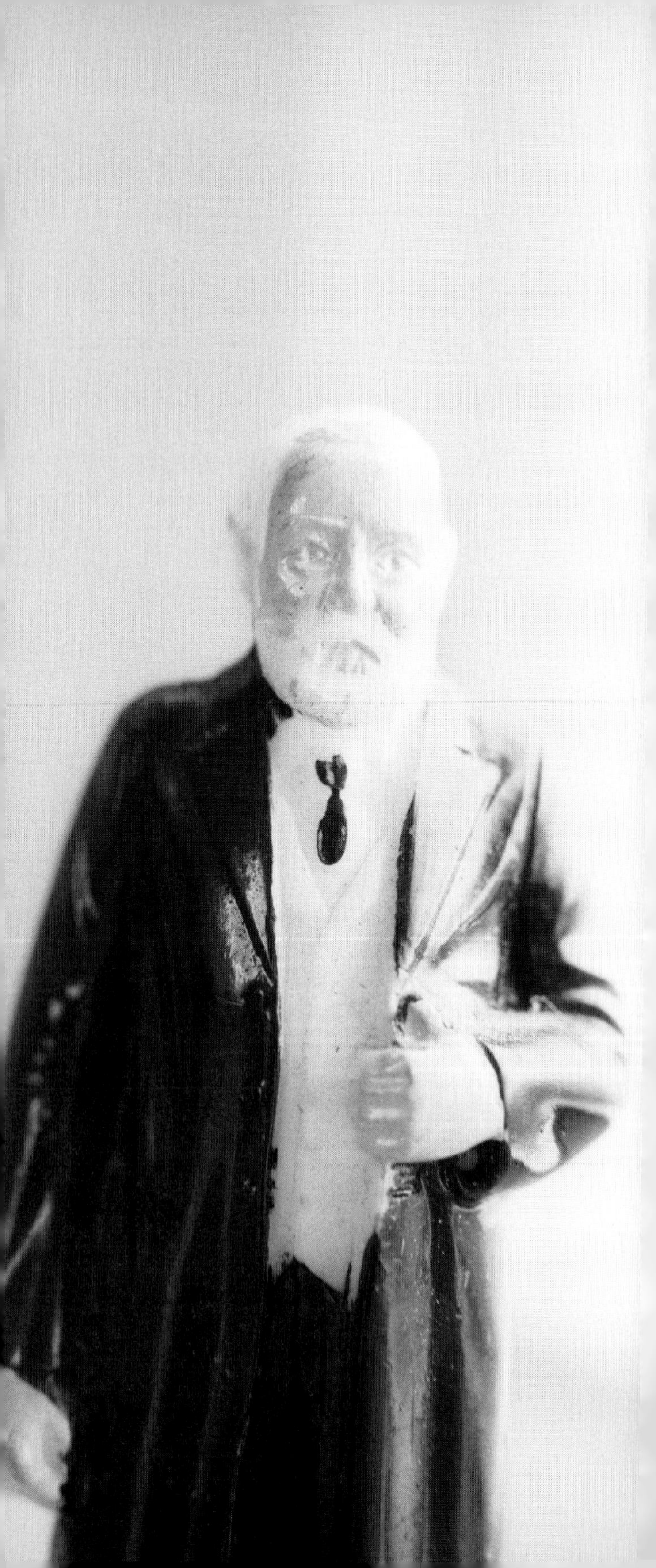

HARRISON

23rd, 1889–93

Benjamin Harrison's handshake was like a wilted petunia.

In appearance he was short—about 5 feet 7 inches—red-bearded, blue-eyed, and fair; his stocky frame moved quickly. He was the last president to wear a beard while in office.

Harrison's ancestor, Thomas Harrison, tried King Charles I and signed his death warrant. On the restoration of the monarchy, he was beheaded, and his descendants emigrated to the United States.

Grandson of our ninth president, Harrison was a cautious, frigid, unimaginative little man. He had the reputation of being distant and was known as The Human Iceberg.

Illness and depression caused his wife, Carrie, to imagine that Harrison was falling in love with her niece, the widow Mary Lord Dimmick. After his wife's death from tuberculosis, Harrison married her niece. He was healthy and vigorous and enjoyed again the pleasures of fatherhood.

Harrison is the first president whose voice was recorded, on a phonograph cylinder in 1889.

In April 1891, Harrison became the first president to travel across the United States by train. He made the trip of 10,000 miles to the Pacific Coast and back in thirty-one days, during which he delivered 140 addresses. They were remarkable for felicity of expression and showed his ability to make a large number of short speeches a day, each having a distinct thought. In these qualities he was not surpassed by any man of his time.

He had electricity installed in the White House but he and his wife would not touch the light switches for fear of electrocution and would often sleep with the lights on.

His death was quiet and painless, with a gradual sinking until the end came, which was marked by a single gasp for breath as life departed from his body. His final words, *Doctor... my lungs.*

d. March 13, 1901 (Indianapolis, Indiana), at 61, of pneumonia.

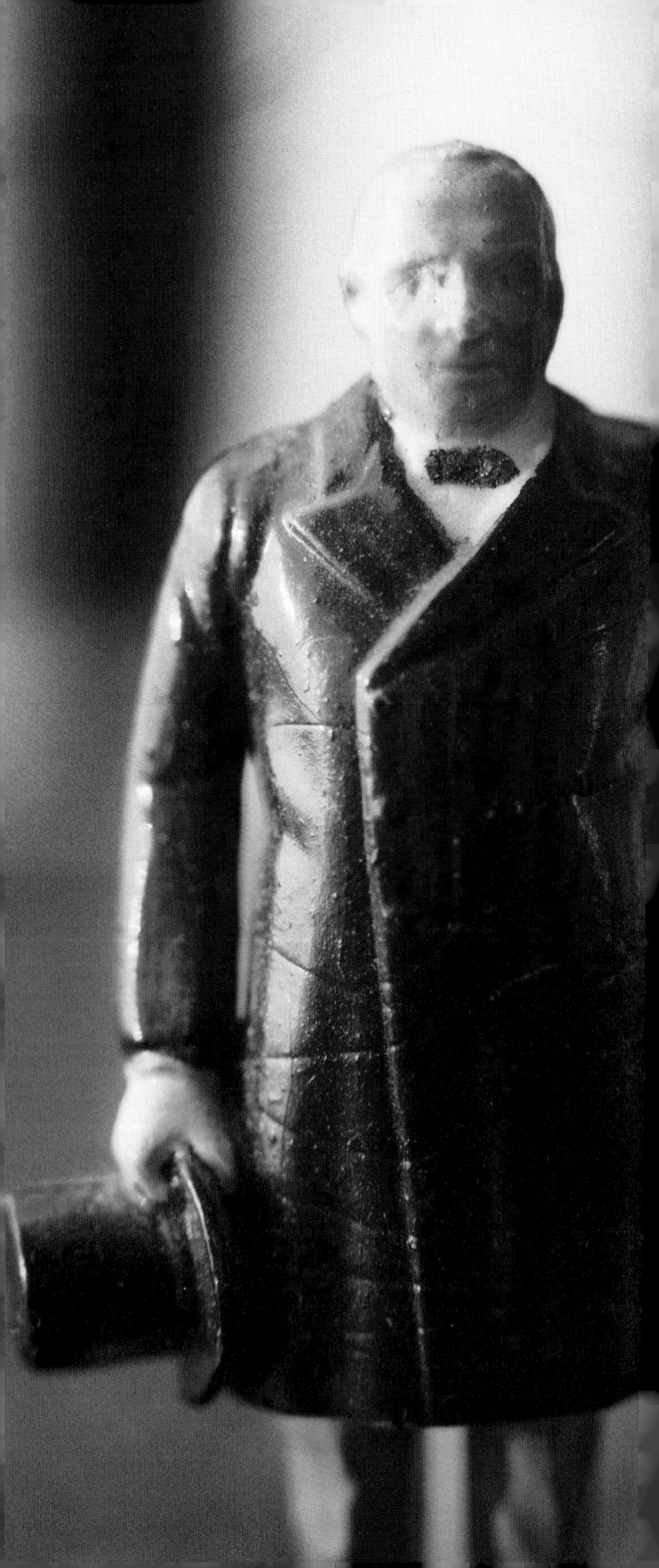

McKINLEY

25th, 1897–1901

A gentle, dignified man, William McKinley was one of the early few who frankly sought the presidency and finally achieved his goal. He was 5 feet 7 inches—shorter than the average man.

He was the last Civil War veteran to become president and the third martyred president within the space of thirty-six years. Anarchist Leon F. Czolgosz shot McKinley in the abdomen because, he said, I thought it would be a good thing for the country to kill the president. I didn't believe one man should have so much service and another man should have none.

McKinley had told Chicago newspaper publisher, H.H. Kohlsaat, that they were trying to force him into declaring war with Spain. As he said this, He broke down and wept as I have never seen anyone weep in my life. His whole body was shaken with convulsive sobs. He asked me when we got into the light if his eyes were red, and I told him they were, but if he blew his nose very hard just as he entered, the redness of his eyes would be attributed to that cause. He did so, and I never heard any of the guests, with whom I mingled freely, comment on the fact that the president had been crying.

To save wear and tear on his right hand at receptions, he developed what came to be called the McKinley Grip. In receiving lines, he would smile as a man came by, take his right hand and squeeze it warmly before his own hand got caught in a hard grip, hold the man's elbow with his left hand, and then swiftly pull him along and be ready to beam on the next guest. Once he clasped 1,900 hands in nineteen minutes, or about one per second. He was always in condition because he was always shaking somebody's hand.

McKinley's wife, Ida, was subject to headaches and seizures. In order to attend to her, if necessary, McKinley broke tradition and sat next to her at official dinners. For example, one evening at dinner with William Taft, a peculiar hissing sound came from Ida. McKinley quickly

picked up a napkin, dropped it over her face, and continued talking. Ida recovered a few moments later, and resumed her part in the conversation where she had left off.

His last words were whispered to his wife, *Nearer my God to Thee, nearer to Thee.* At 3:30 pm, in the afternoon of September 14, 1901, after five minutes of silence across the nation, numerous bands across the United States played the hymn.

d. September 14, 1901 (Buffalo, New York), at 58, of gangrene.

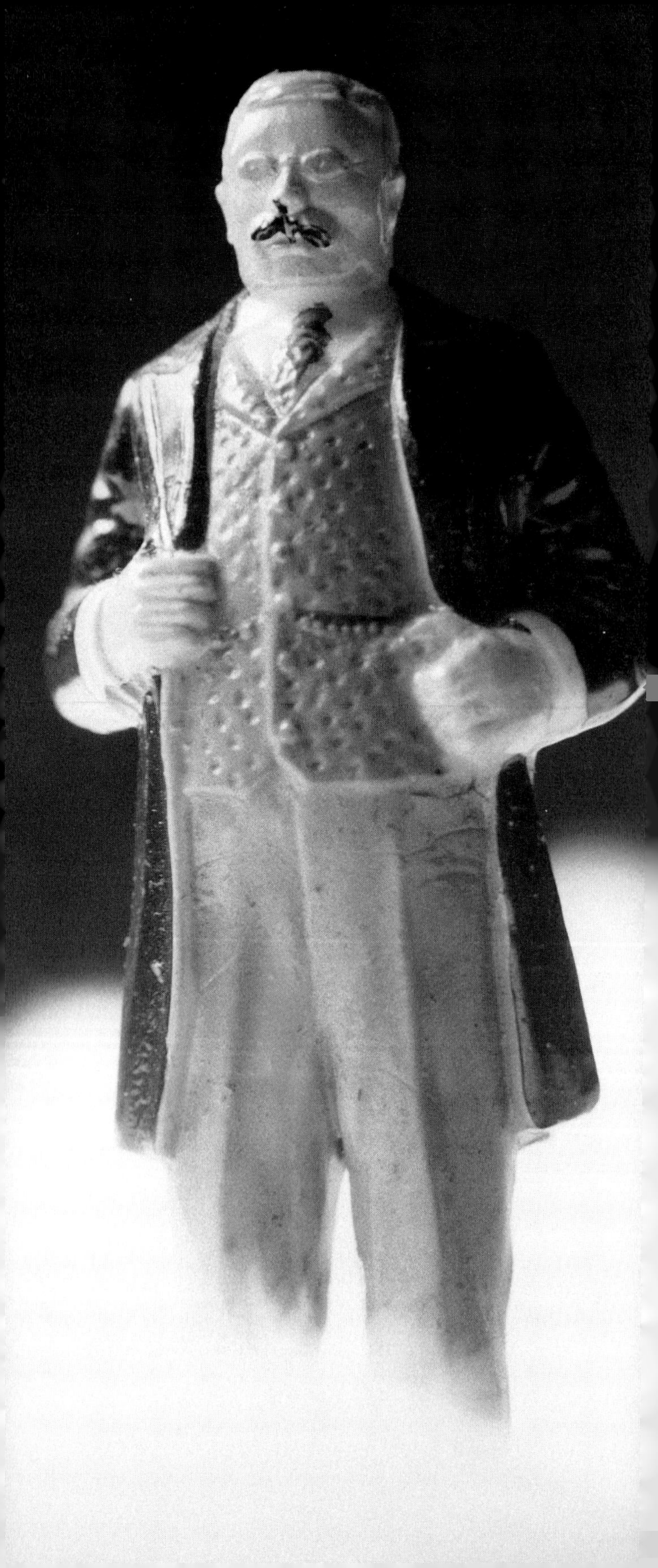

ROOSEVELT

26th, 1901–09

Theodore Roosevelt was an artist of power. Forty-two when he took office, he was the youngest of the nation's chief executives. He weighed 250 pounds. He built up his body and invented the strenuous life.

The public knew of his boxing, wrestling, jujitsu, tennis, hiking, and riding, but not of his sclerotic arteries or of the blindness in his left eye, injured in a White House boxing match. People were drawn by his energy and joy, qualities he possessed in quantities rarely found in persons over the age of eight.

A newspaper wrote: The president rode horseback ninety-eight miles in one day, and was able to sit down comfortably for a late dinner. What's the use of Congress trying to spank a man like that?

Roosevelt said, Our first duty, our most important work, is setting our own house in order. We must be true to ourselves, or else, in the long run, we shall be false to all others. When a friend advised him to rein in his oldest daughter, Alice, he answered, I can be president—or—I can attend to Alice. It was, however, impossible to do both.

In 1912, Roosevelt's campaign manager wrote: I have seen him eat a whole chicken and drink four large glasses of milk at one meal.

Roosevelt was the first president to have his life chronicled by motion pictures.

He was the first president to fly.

He had the family crest, Qui plantavit curabit, tattooed on an undisclosed part of his body.

Alice said of Roosevelt, he longed to be the bride at every wedding, the corpse at every funeral, and the baby at every christening.

At 10:30 in the evening, January 5, 1919, Roosevelt had the odd sensation that his heart and breathing had stopped. He knew they hadn't and he told his wife, Edith, I am perfectly all right but I have a curious feeling. Edith recorded in her diary: At four A.M., T. stopped breathing. Had had sweet sound sleep.

Death had to take him sleeping, said vice president Thomas R. Marshall, for if Roosevelt had been awake there would have been a fight.

The last words uttered by Roosevelt were to his servant Amos after he had retired, and they were: *Please put out that light, James.*

d. January 6, 1919 (Sagamore Hill, Long Island, New York), at 60, from a pulmonary embolism.

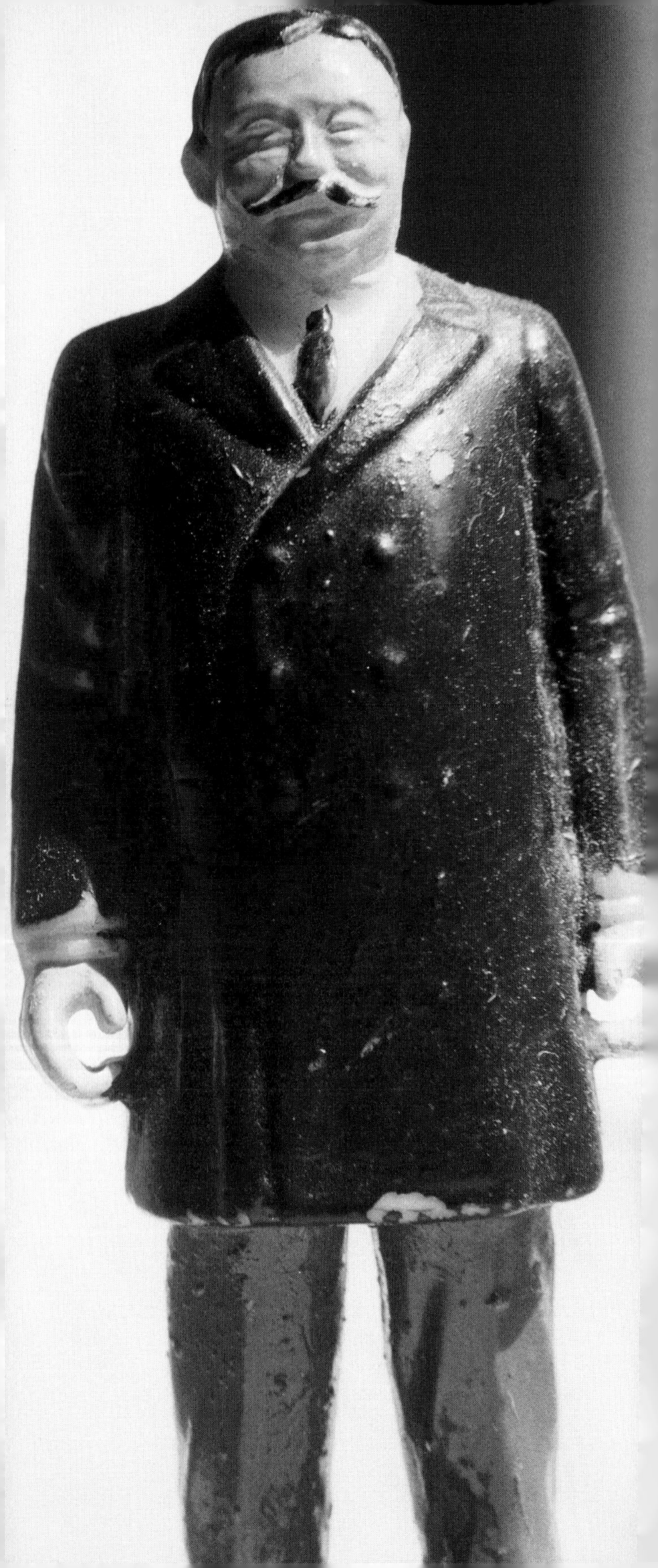

TAFT

27th, 1909–19

Throughout his life, William Howard Taft's weight generally paralleled his unhappiness. Taft was 5 feet 11 1/2 inches tall. He weighed 243 pounds when he graduated from college. He weighed 335–340 pounds when he left the White House.

The one thing that Taft never asked of his portraitists was to slim him down. When told his likeness made him look pudgy, Taft answered, But I am pudgy.

He consumed eight-course breakfasts.

He was indolent, irresolute, dependent, and undone by opposition and criticism. Taft thrived by anchoring himself to intimates and striving to please them by doing what they thought best. Taft's course had been set by a voracious, controlling wife, Nellie, and overbearing mother.

Through his mother, Taft was a seventh cousin twice removed of Richard Nixon.

Taft only ever wanted to be Chief Justice on the Supreme Court. When asked about his time on the Supreme Court and as president, Chief Justice Taft allegedly remarked, I don't remember that I ever was president.

Even during his term, Taft persisted in addressing Theodore Roosevelt as Mr. President. Roosevelt continued to object, and Taft repeatedly overruled him, declaring that he always thought of Roosevelt as president.

His voice was tenor. This startled audiences, who expected a deep bass from so big a man.

Taft had severe obstructive sleep apnea—a disease that steals energy, stamina, intellect, patience, forgiveness, and life. Taft wrote that he developed a pain in the joint of the big toe due I suppose to standing so long when shaking hands in one position. Doctor suspects a little gout, but this is too aristocratic for me.

Taft was the first president to ride in an automobile.

Taft owned a Holstein cow, Pauline Wayne, which he let graze freely on the White House lawn. Pauline was the last cow to live at the White House.

Although his general health declined, Taft was his normal, alert self as December 1929 ended. By the end of January 1930, he was hallucinating. By the end of February 1930, he was intermittently comatose. He was dead on March 8.

d. March 8, 1930 (Washington, DC), at 72, of a heart ailment.

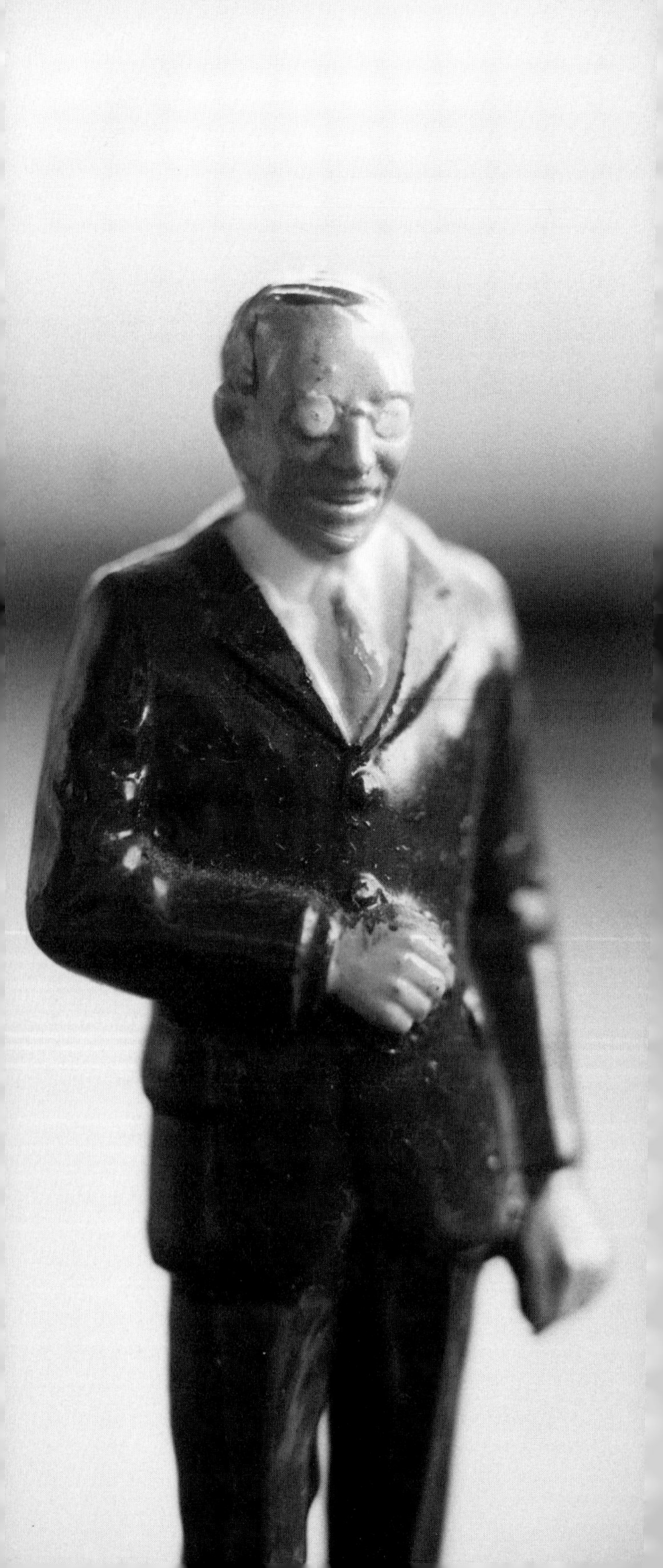

WILSON

28th, 1913–21

Thomas Woodrow Wilson had iron-gray hair, a determined thrust of jaw, and slate-blue eyes behind glittering, rimless glasses. His face was out of proportion: there was too much below the eyeglasses, too little above. He had a beaked nose, protuberant ears, and a loose, meaty upper lip. His ugliness obsessed him.

He never smoked, but decay had mottled his teeth, so that when he smiled, patches of yellow, brown, and blue with glints of gold were exhibited. On his face was a habitual astringence, but he could suddenly confront a person or a camera with a momentary expression of lover-like understanding and affection.

Colonel Edward M. House recorded in his diary: I never knew a man whose general appearance changed so much from hour to hour. He is one of the most difficult and complex characters I have ever known. According to Sigmund Freud, Wilson's single consistent trait was a hatred of nearly all men on earth. He did, in fact, greatly love himself always.

All his life, he insisted on his intensity and his strong passions. But at the age of twenty-eight he was almost certainly a virgin. His pleasures were all connected with the use of his mouth. Men of ordinary physique and discretion, wrote Wilson in 1908, cannot be president and live, if the strain be not somehow relieved.

Wilson's handshake was described as a ten-cent pickled mackerel in brown paper.

His career as a lawyer is quickly recounted: he never had a client.

He did not learn the alphabet until he was nine and could not read until he was twelve. It is likely that he had dyslexia. He was the last president to write his own speeches. He composed them on a Multiplex typewriter.

Wilson enjoyed being president. He was driven around in his car by his secret agents to apprehend speeders. Wilson asked the attorney general if he had the power to give speeding tickets. He was told no.

Wilson suffered a catastrophic, disabling stroke in September 1919 and his condition was hidden from his cabinet, from the vice president and, of course, from the public. The man who lived on was a pathetic invalid, a querulous old man full of rage and tears, hatred and self-pity. He remained, in title, President of the United States until March 4, 1921; but during the last eighteen months of his administration, his wife, Edith, was in large measure the chief executive. Edith Boling Galt has been called the First Lady President.

Women received the right to vote with the passing of the 19th amendment in 1920.

Wilson was dependent upon women to an extraordinary degree. The only president buried in Washington, DC, his last word was *Edith*. He died in his sleep.

d. February 3, 1924 (Washington, DC), at 67, of paralysis and stroke.

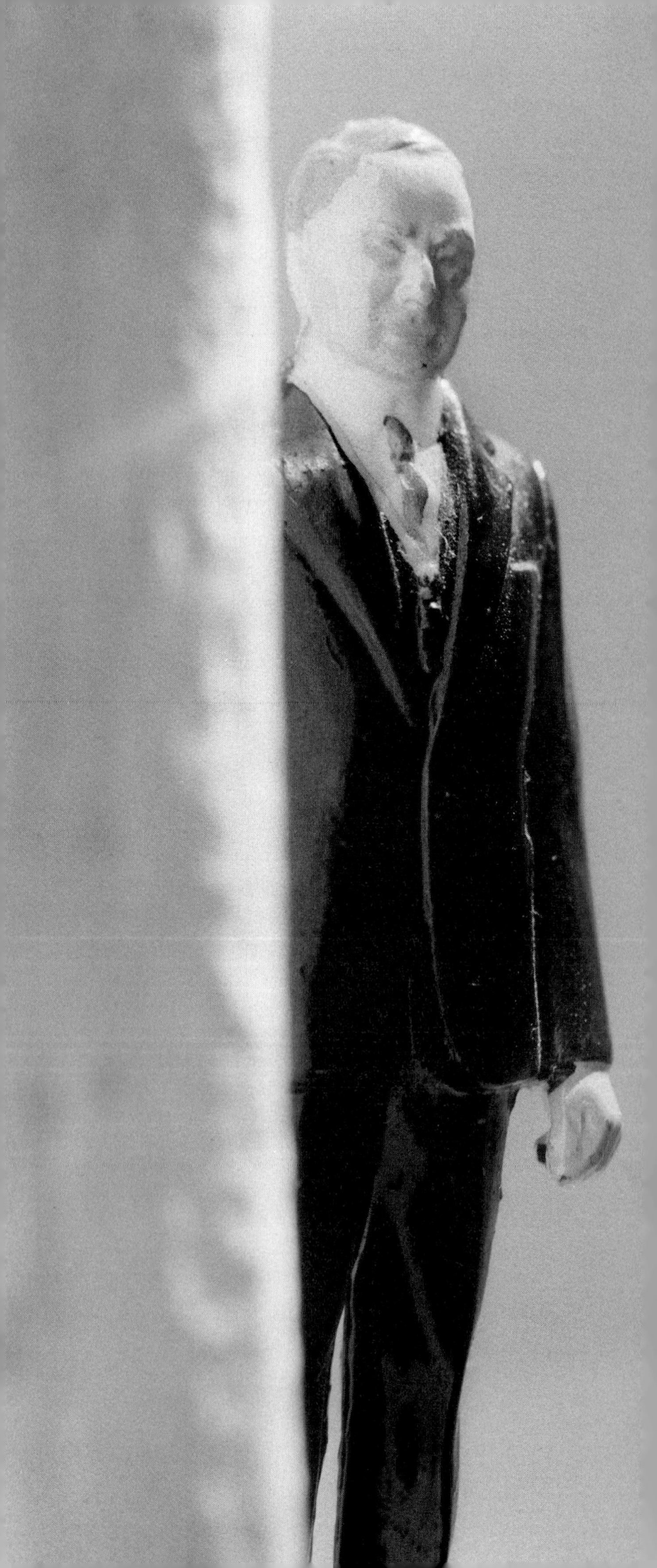

HARDING

29th, 1921–23

Warren Gamaliel Harding looked like a president. He was superbly handsome, big-framed, with large, wide-set eyes and a pleasant, resonant voice. Behind the statesman-like exterior was a man who remained forever insecure about his ability to lead.

The passage of the Nineteenth Amendment in 1920 made it possible for his wife, Florence, to become the first First Lady to vote for her husband. But, Malcolm Gladwell coined the phrase the Warren Harding Error to describe what happens when our first impressions are so powerful that they cloud our better judgment. Florence worried incessantly about Harding's grasp of events and had the cabinet report to her.

When Republican leaders called on Harding to deny his Negro history, he said: How should I know whether or not one of my ancestors might have jumped the fence.

He was a highly skilled hand shaker who genuinely loved people.

Knowing that his political and home lives would be ruined by revelations that he adulterously fathered a child, Harding tried to convince Nan Britton to terminate the pregnancy. He offered her a bottle of medication (Dr. Humphrey's No. 11 tablets) that his wife took. Britton declined and, on October 22, 1919, delivered the girl who had been conceived in the Senate Office Building. Through the pregnancy and afterwards, Harding never abandoned Britton.

H.L. Mencken wrote about Harding's English, or Gamalielese, as he called it: It reminds me of a string of wet sponges; it reminds me of tattered washing on the line; it reminds me of stale bean soup, of college yells, of dogs barking idiotically through endless nights. It is so bad that a sort of grandeur creeps into it.

Harding was the first president to speak over the radio.

Harding used tobacco in all forms. He had two cigars a day, interspersed with a pipe and an occasional cigarette. He also chewed tobacco. To a White House visitor he admitted, I knew that this job would be too much for me.

In 1923, Harding was a sick man. He had stomach troubles, lung troubles, heart troubles, and friend troubles. He died because it was the best thing to do.

Harding did more than any other president to preserve the Constitution of the United States. He removed that great document from the files of the State Department, where it was rotting, and put it in a protective glass case.

His last words were to his wife, *That's good. Go on. Read some more.*

d. August 2, 1923 (San Francisco, California), at 57, of sudden death.

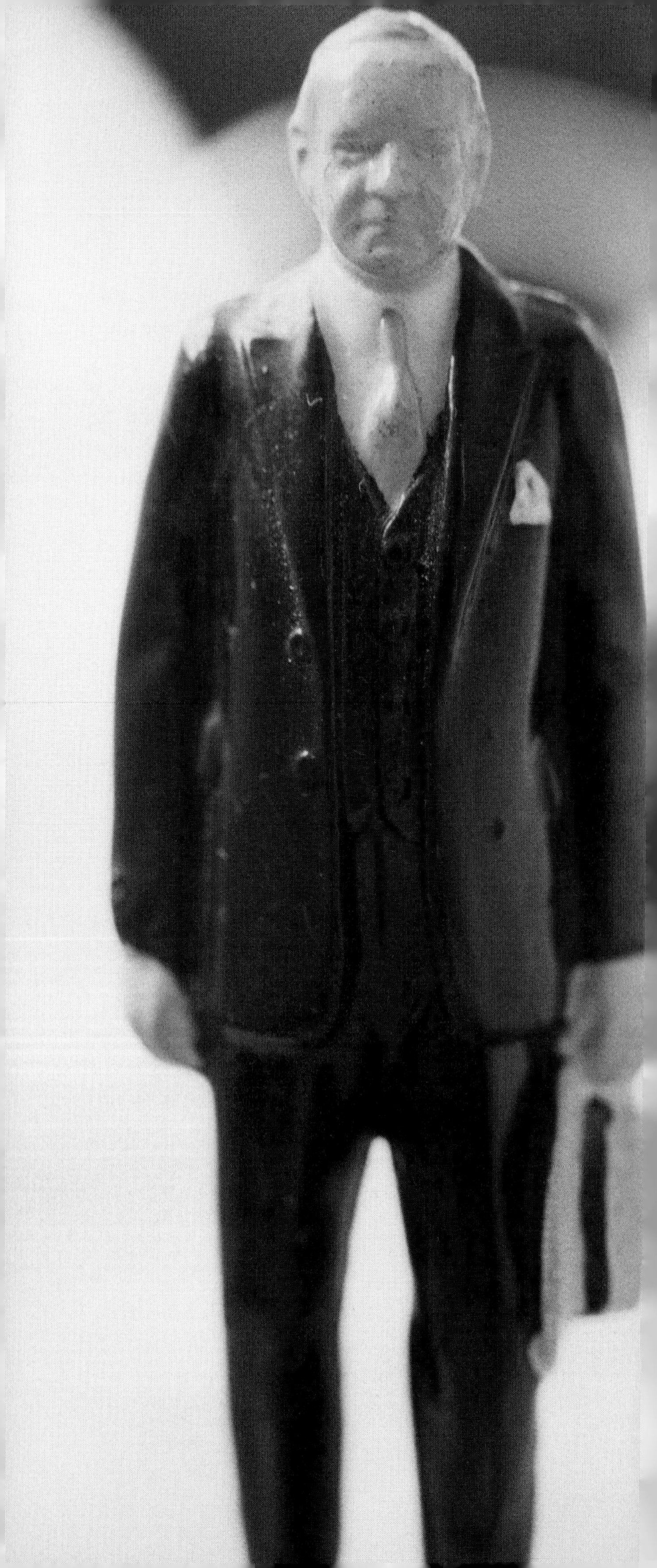

COOLIDGE

30th, 1923–29

A Harvard professor observed that Calvin Coolidge was a small, hatchet-faced, colorless man, with a tight-shut, thin-lipped mouth; very chary of words, but with a gleam of understanding in his pretty keen eye. In appearance Coolidge was splendidly null, apparently deficient in red corpuscles, with a peaked, wire-drawn expression.

His voice was likened to a quack.

Coolidge was agoraphobic and could not stand public speaking. When I was a little fellow, Coolidge recalled, as long ago as I can remember, I would go into a panic if I heard strange voices in the kitchen. Everytime I meet a stranger, I've got to go through that old kitchen door.

Recognizing the contrast between himself and his gregarious wife, Grace Goodhue, who taught at a school for the deaf in Northampton, Massachusetts, Coolidge remarked, Having taught the deaf to hear, Miss Goodhue might perhaps cause the mute to speak. Coolidge was the first president to broadcast an inaugural address.

Coolidge slept eleven hours a day. He went to bed at 10 P.M., got up between 7 and 9 A.M., and always took an afternoon nap lasting two to four hours.

He proudly admitted that his mother was dark because of mixed Indian ancestry. Her maiden name was Moor.

Coolidge hated being photographed, but he was one of the most frequently snapped men of his era. He was once asked how he got his exercise: Having my picture taken, he replied.

A few days after Coolidge entered the White House, he wrote to Jim Lucey, a cobbler from his hometown, I want you to know, he said, that if it were not for you I should not be here and I want to tell you how much I love you.

Upon leaving the White House, he prided himself on being in better physical condition than when he entered it, and better physically than most of his predecessors when they retired from the office. Coolidge died of a sudden

heart attack in his dressing room at his modest estate, The Beeches. He was found lying on his back, with a calm expression on his face, as if he had died without pain or suffering. He was in his shirtsleeves.

Jim Lucey was heartbroken. The old man stood in his shop, pipe in hand, arm resting on the counter, and recalled the days when he and Calvin Coolidge used to exchange their views upon life. I'm sorry. I'm sorry. He was the best friend I ever had, said the cobbler of the former president.

d. January 5, 1933 (Northampton, Massachusetts), at 60, of a coronary thrombosis.

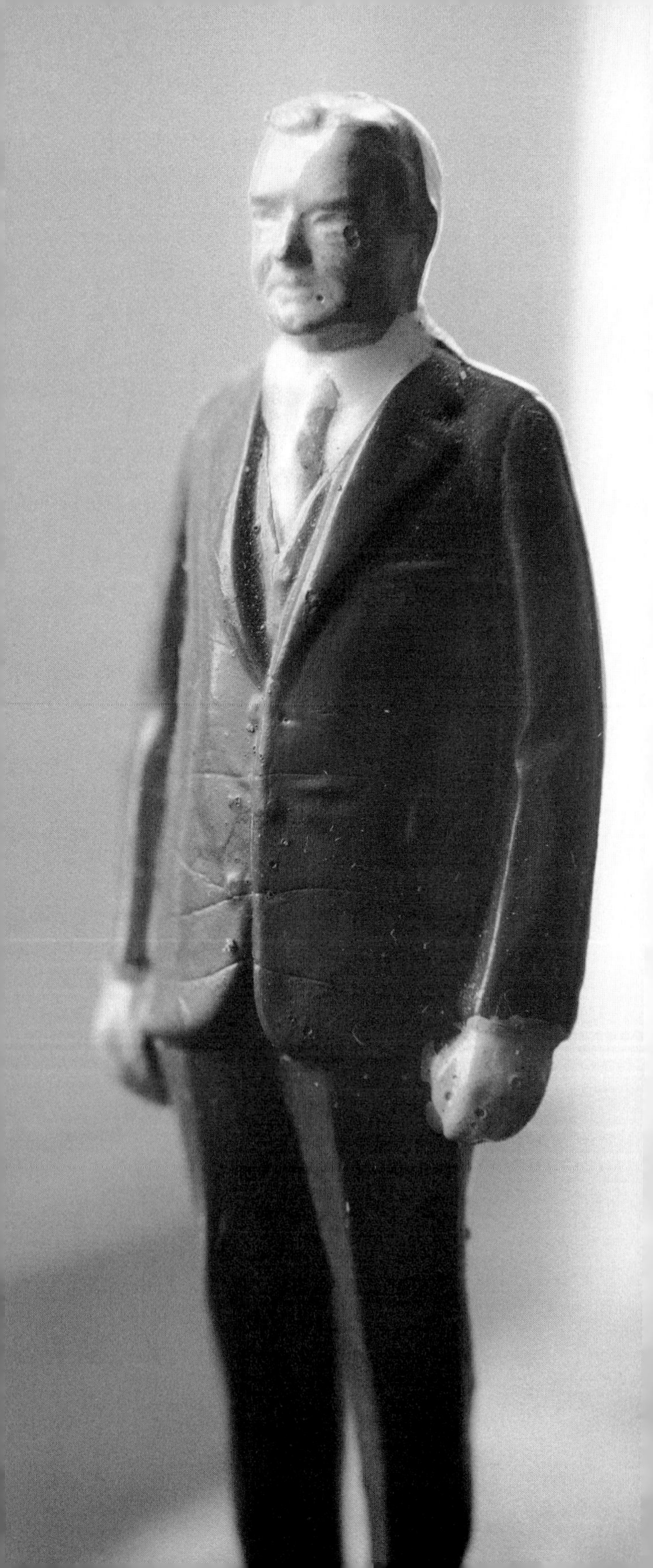

HOOVER

31st, 1929–33

Tall, sturdy, and energetic, with broad shoulders, hazel eyes, a round face, and straight, grayish-brown hair, Herbert Clark Hoover refused to allow photographs while smoking cigars.

He was the first president born west of the Mississippi River. His parents were poor, and he was orphaned at nine, but he amassed a fortune as a mine engineer and owner. His personal estate was estimated to be worth $4 million by 1914.

He once described himself as a square doodler.

The word Hooverize was coined to suggest saving, substituting, practicing self-denial, and thus helping win the war. Newspapers wrapped around the body for warmth were Hoover blankets. Cars that had broken down and were pulled by mule teams were Hoover wagons. The ubiquitous empty pocket turned inside out was a Hoover flag, and unappetizing jackrabbits were called Hoover hogs. In his attacks on waste, he instituted an impressive sequence of meetings and conferences (his own estimate was more than 3,000). In 1960, he wrote 55,952 letters with his staff.

Hoover's wife, Lou Henry, was the first First Lady to speak on the radio and give regular interviews. In the White House, the Hoovers often spoke to each other in Mandarin when they wanted to foil potential eavesdroppers. Through his mother, Hoover was an eighth cousin once removed of Richard Nixon.

Annual receptions amounted to a rapidly moving assembly line of thousands of handshakes. He said, And often enough my hand would be so swollen for days after that I could not write with it.

Active to the end of his days—he employed six secretaries to handle his correspondence—Hoover died at the age of ninety. Only one other president, John Adams, had lived as long.

Death came in his suite on the thirty-first floor of the Waldorf Towers. The first word of Hoover's passing came

in a terse, handwritten note on Waldorf stationery from his personal physician, Dr. Michael J. Lepore. It gave only name, date, and time. Its text: President Hoover. Oct. 20, 1964. Time: 11:35 A.M.

d. October 20, 1964 (Washington, DC), at 90, of a severe gastrointestinal hemorrhage.

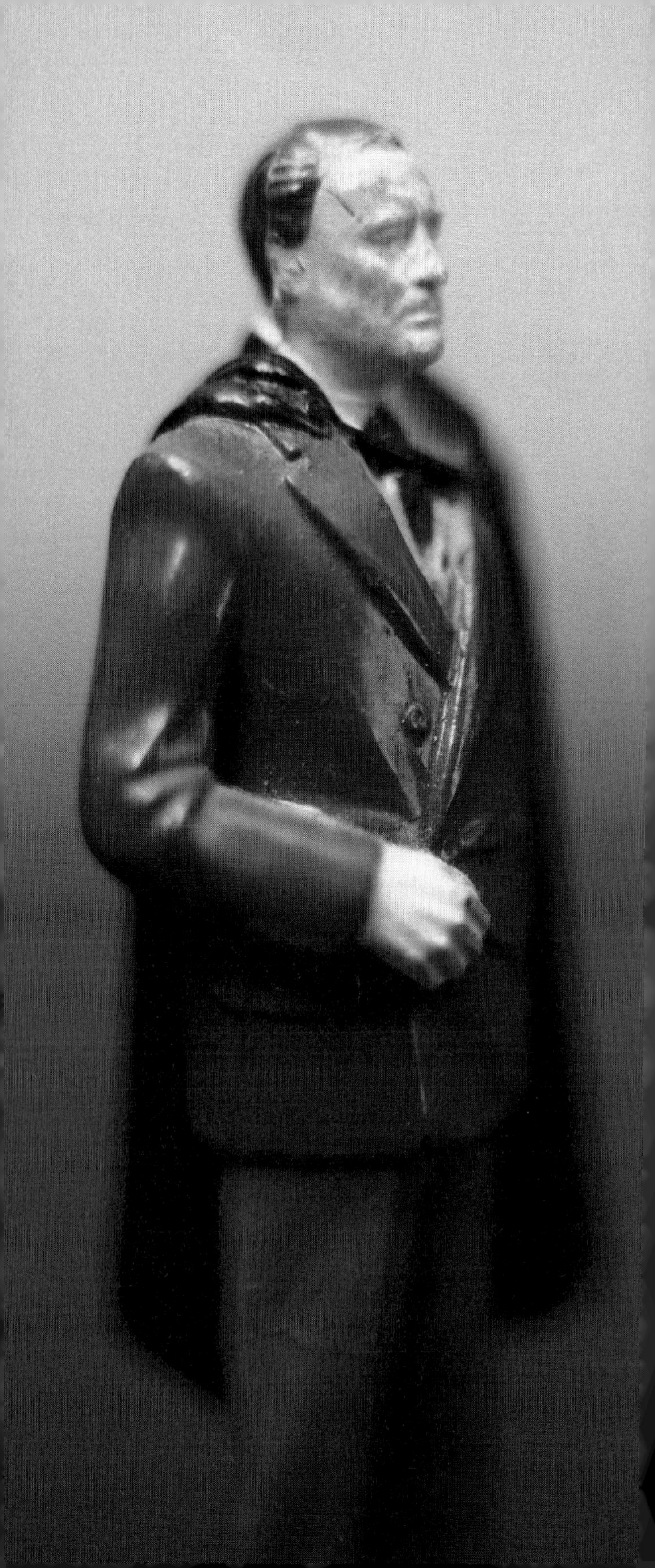

ROOSEVELT

32nd, 1933–45

Franklin Delano Roosevelt, Woodrow Wilson proclaimed, was the handsomest young giant I have ever seen. Dr. Draper wrote: He has such courage, such ambition, and yet at the same time such an extraordinarily sensitive emotional mechanism.

In the fall of 1900, FDR entered Harvard and went all out to make the football team. He was turned down when he weighed in at a brittle 146 pounds. He became, instead, a cheerleader.

FDR's side of the family pronounced Roosevelt as in rose.

Eleanor Roosevelt thought FDR's polio, contracted in 1921, a turning point that proved a blessing in disguise for it gave him strength and courage he had not had before. He would be forced to crawl from room to room, to pull the dead weight of his lower limbs up flights of stairs, to submit to being carried about like a child, and to carry papers and books in his teeth. Few Americans were ever aware of FDR's disability. This was due in large part to the cooperation of members of the press, who almost always photographed him from the waist up.

FDR had the longest administration of any president—12 years, 1 month and 8 days.

His main health problem, starting around November 1944, was anorexia.

The famed Roosevelt smile drove some men to fury. Others found it irresistible. To his critics it characterized his insincerity and deviousness—traits even his friends admitted he had.

FDR had an affair with Eleanor's secretary, Lucy Mercer, from 1918 until his death in 1945, while Eleanor for many years carried on a loving relationship with a woman named Lorena Hickok.

FDR appointed Madame Secretary Frances Perkins, the first woman to hold a Cabinet post thus becoming the first woman to enter the presidential line of succession.

FDR was the first to fly while president.

In 1945, after sitting for his portrait in his small cottage, Roosevelt complained of a terrific headache, lost consciousness, and died. All over the world people said the president had died, and nobody asked which president, or president of what, because to them FDR had been The President.

FDR's arteries were so atherosclerotic that embalmers could not get a needle into them.

d. April 12, 1945 (Warm Springs, Georgia), at 63, of a cerebral hemorrhage less than six months after being elected to a fourth term in office.

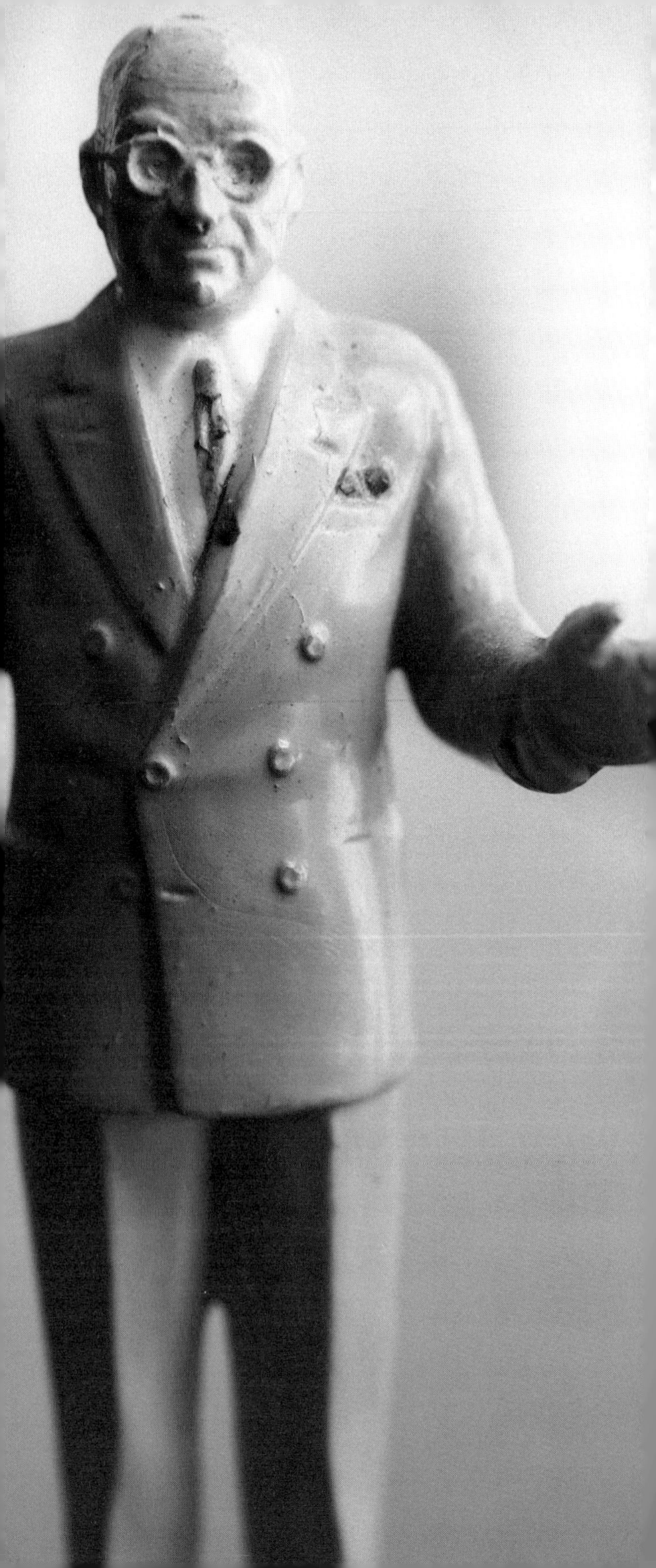

TRUMAN

33rd, 1945–53

Harry S. Truman's ramrod posture made him recognizable even with his back to the camera. He was a war president, a postwar president, and a cold-war president.

Truman always drove too fast.

He was afflicted from boyhood with poor eyesight and he was left-handed but forced to use his right. By the time he was fourteen, he had read every book in the public library at Independence, Missouri. He married Bess, his sweetheart from the fifth grade. Truman was the last president not to earn a college degree.

When a peach pit lodged in his throat, his mother saved his life by quick action: She pushed the pit down his throat with her finger.

He was briefed about the atomic bomb for only thirty minutes, after he had become president.

Truman gave strong approval for a judicial process and said in support of the Nuremberg Trials: Never again can men say, I was following orders. And never again can men in power give such orders.

Had dinner by myself tonight, Truman noted in 1949. Barnett in tails and white tie pulls out my chair, pushes me up to the table. John in tails and white tie brings me a fruit cup. Barnett takes the empty cup. John comes in with a napkin and silver crumb tray—there are no crumbs but John has to brush them off the table anyway. I take the hand bath in the finger bowl and go back to work. He was the first president to be paid a salary of $100,000.

Truman could play the piano for foreign dignitaries one day, and the next he could propose legislation so visionary that it would not be enacted for a decade—such as the Civil Rights Act of 1964 and Medicare of 1965.

He said, I've got the most awful responsibility a man ever had. If you fellows ever pray, pray for me. He wrote in his journal on January 6, 1947: This great white jail is a hell of a place in which to be alone. The floors pop and crack all night long. Anyone with imagination can see old Jim Buchanan walking up and down worrying about

conditions not of his making. Then there's Van Buren who inherited a terrible mess from his predecessor, as did poor old James Madison. Of course Andrew Johnson was the worst mistreated of any of them. So the tortured souls who were and are misrepresented in history are the ones who come back.

d. December 26, 1972 (Kansas City, Missouri), at 88, of heart failure and pulmonary congestion.

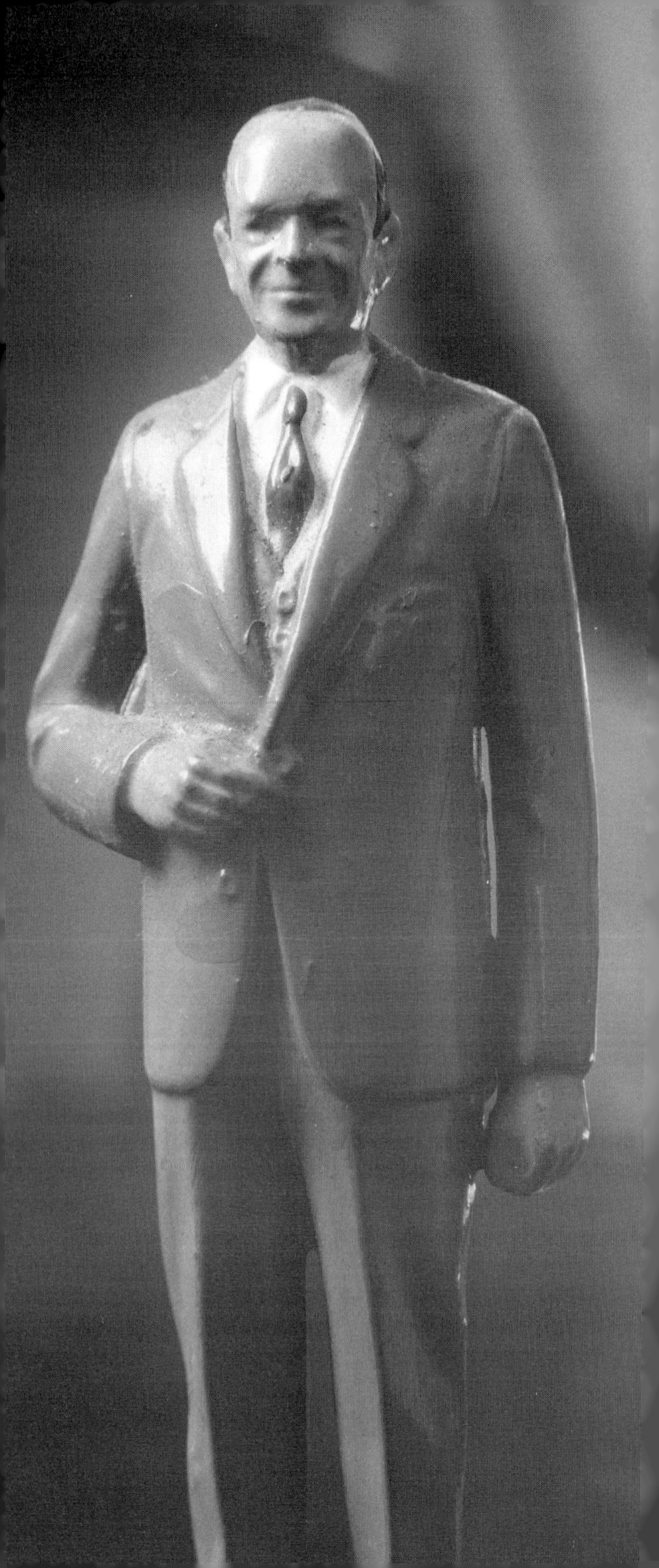

EISENHOWER

34th, 1953–61

Dwight David Eisenhower was bald.

His prominent forehead and broad mouth made his head seem larger than it was. He had a wonderfully expressive face, and it was impossible for him to conceal his feelings. He was only a little above average in height and weight.

Failing to discover anything about him that portended greatness, journalists portrayed him as a good man. Eisenhower and Mamie became engaged on St. Valentine's Day, 1916. Like the people in the old fairy tales, they lived happily ever after. His beliefs were those of Main Street.

He was the third regular army man to become president. He was the first president to be born in Texas and the first of German ancestry. He was the first president to hold a pilot's license. And he was the first to hold a televised news conference.

You're on pages one, two and three of every newspaper, Louis Marx, the Toy King, said to Eisenhower in 1946. You're the political Coca-Cola. In 1959, Robert Woodruff, president of the Coca-Cola Company, scolded Eisenhower for appearing in a photograph sipping Coke from a bottle through a straw—a sissy way to imbibe. Eisenhower responded, When I tip up a bottle of Coca-Cola for a good drink it lasts only seconds—with a straw, a lot of talk and more walking, I was able to contact more photographers and newspaper correspondents.

In March 1949, Eisenhower's physician advised he cut his smoking from four packs to one pack of cigarettes per day. Eisenhower decided that counting his cigarettes was worse than not smoking at all. Frequently asked how he quit, he said, all he did was put smoking out of his mind. It helped, he would add with a grin, to develop a scornful attitude toward those weaklings who did not have the will power to break their enslavement. I nursed to the utmost... my ability to sneer. His motto was peace through understanding.

From 1955 to 1968, Eisenhower had seven heart attacks and fourteen cardiac arrests. After the first infarct, his press secretary opened Eisenhower's oxygen tent to ask how much information should be released at the upcoming press conference. Eisenhower was said to have replied that they should tell the public everything. As a result, Dr. Paul Dudley White discussed the president's bowel movements and relevant nursing care, leading to criticisms of indiscretion.

While in hospital, Eisenhower wore red pajamas with five gold stars on the collar.

Eisenhower suffered from Crohn's disease. On the day of his fatal infarct, he ate sausage, bacon, mush, and hotcakes for breakfast and a hamburger with raw onion for lunch. When Eisenhower experienced indigestion after lunch, he blamed the onion.

d. March 28, 1969 (Washington, DC), at 78, of congestive heart failure.

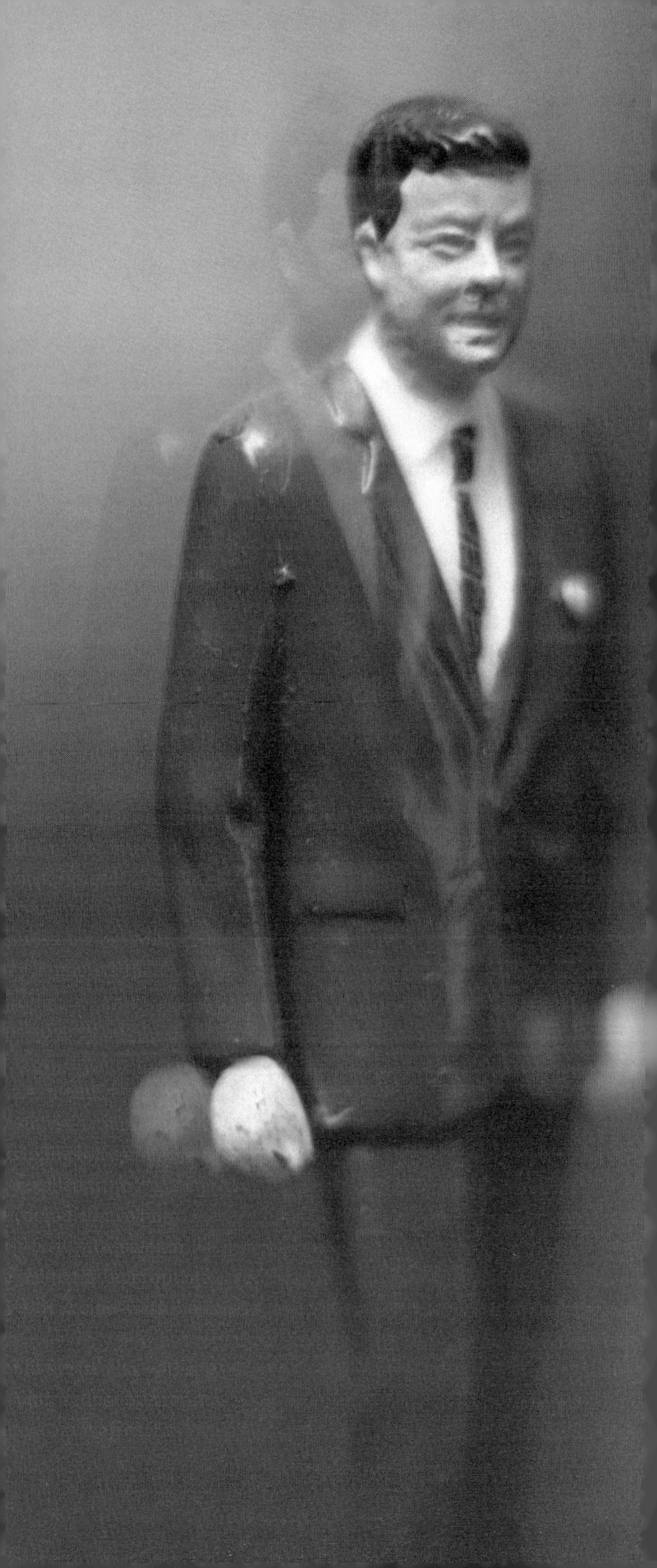

KENNEDY

35th, 1961–63

John Fitzgerald Kennedy had a tan year-round, a symptom of Addison's disease. He liked it: It gives me confidence. Steroids altered the shape of JFK's face and several photographs show a roundness classically known as moon facies.

JFK was hospitalized more than three dozen times and given last rites three times. His mother remembered him as a very, very sick little boy... bed-ridden and elfin-like. In his adolescence, doctors described gastrointestinal symptoms, weight and growth problems, as well as fatigue. Later in life, he suffered from abdominal pain, diarrhea, weight loss, osteoporosis, and migraines, raising the possibility that JFK had celiac disease.

Some of the drugs JFK received in large doses during his first six months in office are described in a Medicine Administration Record: Cortisone—at one extreme, steroid psychosis can result, at the other, a profound sensation of well-being; Lomotil for diarrhea—in toxic doses, can make someone mad as a hatter; Paregoric containing opium; Phenobarbital for diarrhea—a classic downer; testosterone; trasentine for diarrhea—causes giddiness and euphoria; and amphetamines.

JFK dismissed concerns about the medicine, saying, I don't care if it's horse piss. It works. It is thought that he was under the influence of amphetamines when he made his Ich bin ein Berliner speech.

He was absolutely fearless about airplanes, flying anywhere, at any time, in any weather in which he could get aloft, sleeping through anything, scarcely seeming aware that he was off the ground. Yet four persons in his family had died in aircraft accidents.

At age twenty-one, JFK's sister Rosemary tripped at a family visit to the Queen of England. This added insult to injury for Joseph Kennedy who considered her promiscuity a problem. Joseph Kennedy reacted by forcing a pre-frontal lobotomy that proved to be a disaster. She spent the rest of her life in an institution.

In 1963, JFK confided that he got a headache if he went too long without a woman. A fellow congressman observed that traveling with him was like traveling with a bull.

From frame #220 until #224, the Zapruder camera's view is obscured by a road sign. The only part of Kennedy's body visible is his waving hand above it. At frame #312, Kennedy's head jerks down and forward as the bullet strikes the back of his skull, slightly to the right of the midline. In the next frame, the President's head is blown open above the right temple in a horrible pink cloud.

In Dallas, Texas, Lady Bird Johnson said, Suddenly, I found myself face to face with Jackie, in a small hall right outside the operating room. You always think of her or somebody like her as being insulated, protected. She was quite alone. I don't think I ever saw anybody so alone in my life.

Among JFK's endowments—rarely to be found in politicians—was the capacity for cold and critical self-examination. Even so, he injected the presidency with a cosmopolitan glamour and the Kennedy idealism, which made it seem that a more equitable and peaceful world was possible.

d. November 22, 1963 (Dallas, Texas), at 46, by a sniper's bullet fired from the 6th floor Texas School Depository onto his motorcade.

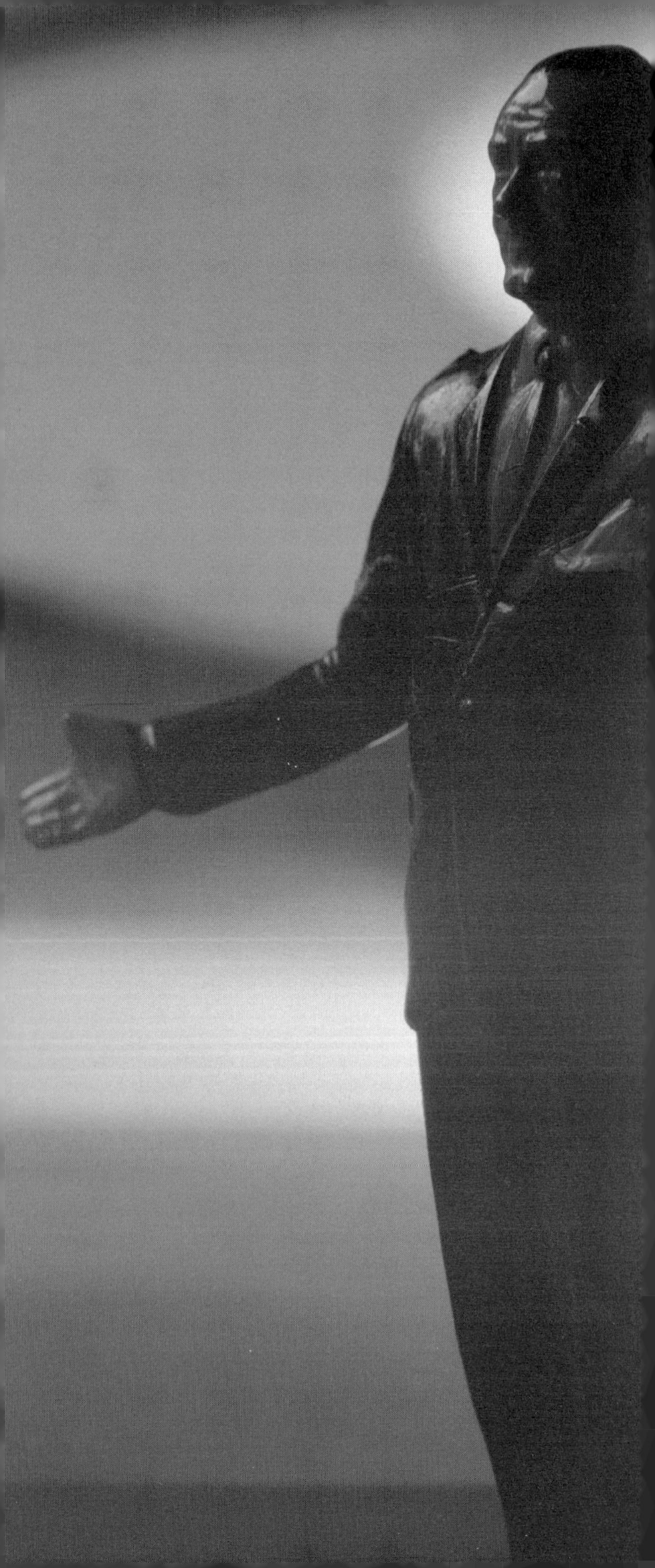

JOHNSON

36th, 1963–69

Lyndon Baines Johnson was 6 feet 3 1/2 inches tall and weighed about 216 pounds. The presidency has made every man who occupied it, no matter how small, bigger than he was, he said, and no matter how big, not big enough for its demands.

He was taught to read by his mother by age four.

White House tapes recorded him asking a photographer to take his family portraits for free, saying he was a very poor man living on a weekly paycheck. LBJ was a multimillionaire, but he still received the photographic portraits gratis.

He insisted that photographers shoot only his left side. LBJ was a man possessed by inner demons.

He was afraid of being alone.

Within ten weeks of their first date, LBJ issued a marriage ultimatum. We either do it now, or we never will, he told Lady Bird. According to journalists Rowland Evans and Robert Novak, LBJ had a treatment he used on people who needed persuasion: He moved in close, his face a scant millimeter from his target, his eyes widening and narrowing, his eyebrows rising and falling. From his pockets poured clippings, memos, statistics. Mimicry, humor, and the genius of analogy rendered the target stunned and helpless.

Lady Bird Johnson was the first First Lady to build and maintain a fortune with her own money. In 1964, she organized the Lady Bird Special—a whistle-stop tour winding 1,628 miles through eight states in four days. She was the first First Lady to campaign for her husband.

LBJ had a small control box installed in the writing desk adjacent to the Oval Office. It contained two buttons, marked Coffee and Fresca. Pushing one of these buttons would summon his military aide with the appropriate drink. His secretary revealed that LBJ would wash and reuse Styrofoam cups.

It was known that LBJ would insist that others accompany him while he used the White House bathroom and continue to discuss official matters or take dictation.

LBJ, on tape: I do not believe I can physically and mentally, uh, carry the responsibilities of the bomb and the world and the negroes and the South, and I know my own limitation, but they think I want great power. All I want is great solace. A little love—that's all I want.

His health was ruined by years of heavy smoking and stress. He died alone. He was found stretched out on his bed, reaching for the telephone.

President Nixon, who presided over the funeral, did not speak but was lauded for his tributes.

d. January 22, 1973 (Stonewall, Texas), at 64, from a third heart attack.

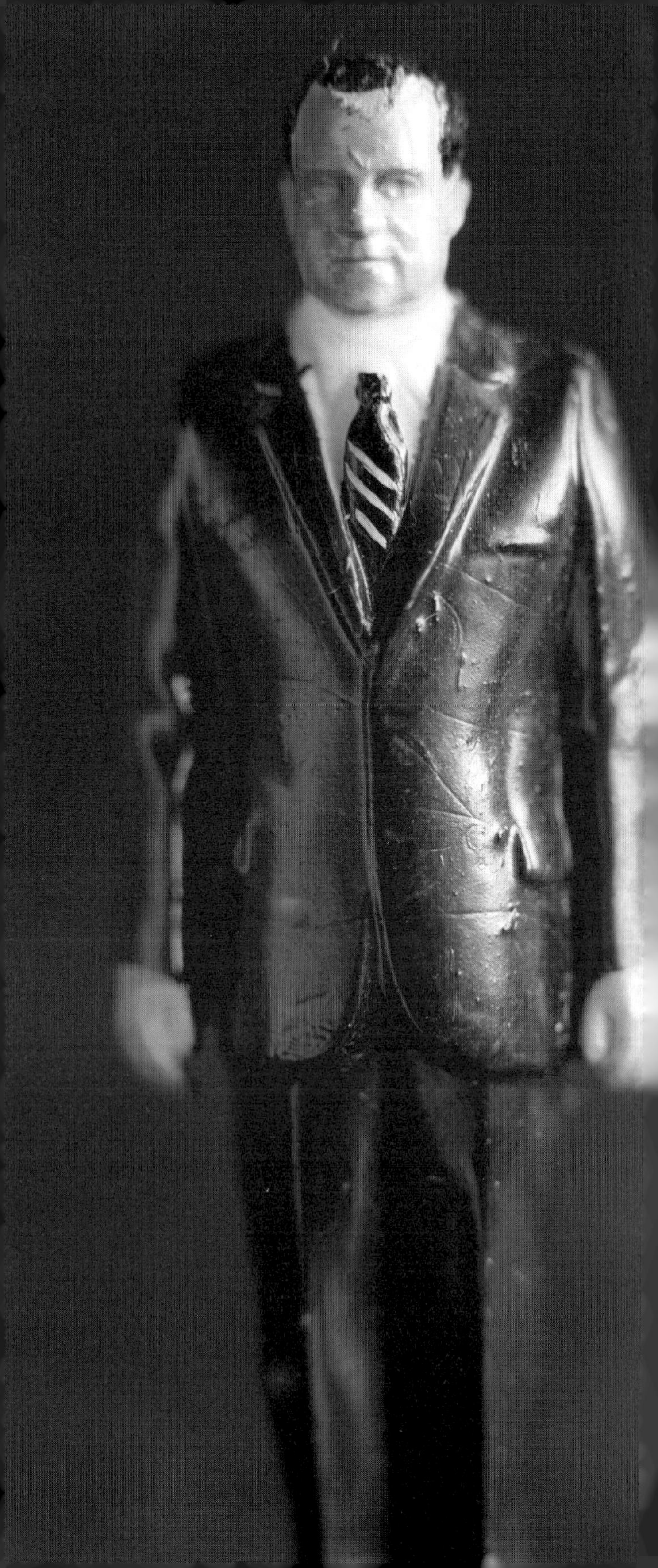

NIXON

37th, 1969–

Richard Milhous Nixon's gestures—the body language, the counting of points on the fingers, the arms up-stretched in the victory sign or sweeping around the body like a matador flicking a cape before a bull—always seemed a little out of sync with what he was saying, as if a soundtrack were running a little ahead of or behind its film.

Norman Rockwell once called Nixon the hardest man I ever had to paint. Nixon fell into the troublesome category of almost good-looking.

Nixon could trace descent from King Edward III of England through an illegitimate line. His was called the Imperial Presidency because, at times, Nixon simply ignored laws. Nixon had a narcissistic and paranoid personality.

He was the first president to visit all fifty states. He made the world's longest long distance phone call to Neil Armstrong on the moon. Americans were shocked to hear the sheer amount of swearing and vicious comments on the president's White House tapes.

Nixon was an alcoholic, and he used Dilantin without a prescription for several years. Long-term use of Dilantin can cause rapid, rhythmic and repetitious involuntary eye movements, ataxia, slurred speech, decreased coordination, mental confusion, and overgrowth of the gums. So bad was the problem in Nixon, that at the height of the Vietnam War the then secretary of defense, James Schlesinger, ordered military commanders not to react to orders from the White House unless they were cleared with him or the secretary of state.

Nixon is the only American to have been elected twice to both the vice presidency and the presidency, and the only president to resign. Furious [eye] blinking was exhibited during his resignation speech on television. Psychologist Joseph Tecce called these mood-triggered, episodic bursts of blinking the Nixon Effect. Key figures that first entered government service in the Nixon White House include George H. W. Bush, Dick Cheney, Henry

Kissinger, Alexander Haig, George Shultz, James Baker, Colin Powell, James Schlesinger, Donald Rumsfeld, and Casper Weinberger.

Nixon was president when Roe v. Wade was written. His favorite breakfast included cottage cheese with ketchup and black pepper.

Nixon asked Pat Ryan to marry him the first night they went out. It's true, she said to one reporter, who asked if she'd refused him, but it's mean to repeat it. By the time the Nixons reached the White House, observers characterized them as people who have lost whatever they once had between them.

Hunter S. Thompson described him as a man who could shake your hand and stab you in the back at the same time. He said, He was a giant in his way.

Nixon suffered a severe stroke in his Park Ridge, New Jersey, home; his last words were yelling out to a housekeeper for help.

d. April 22, 1994 (New York, New York), at 81, of paralysis and swelling of the brain.

SOURCE MATERIAL

This volume was composed, like the *Jefferson Bible*, "by cutting the texts out of the book and arranging them on the pages of a blank book, in a certain order of time or subject." Each phrase was culled from pre-existing presidential letters, biographies, novels, children's books, websites, blogs, accounts, rumors, hearsay, etc., covering the period of American presidential history represented by the Marx Figurines; none of the text herein was written by me.

Print

American Heritage Book of the Presidents and Famous Americans, The. 12-volume edition. New York: Dell Publishing Co., 1967.

Adams, Henry. *The Education of Henry Adams: An Autobiography*. Boston: Houghton Mifflin Company, 1918.

Adams, William Howard. *The Eye of Thomas Jefferson.* Washington: National Gallery of Art, 1976.

Balsiger, David & Charles E. Seller. *The Lincoln Conspiracy*. Los Angeles: Schun Sunn Classic Books, 1977.

Beshchloss, Michael R., ed. *Taking Charge: The Johnson Whitehouse Tapes, 1963-1964*. New York: Simon & Schuster, 1997.

Bishop, Joseph Bucklin. *Theodore Roosevelt's Letters to his Children*. New York: Charles Scribner's Sons, 1919.

Britton, Nan. *The President's Daughter*. New York: Elizabeth Ann Guild, Inc., 1927.

Bromley, Michael L. *William Howard Taft and the First Motoring Presidency, 1909-1913*. New York: McFarland & C, Inc, 2003.

Brode, Fawn M. *Thomas Jefferson: An Intimate History*. New York: W. W. Norton & Company Inc., 1974.

Dallek, Robert. *Hail to the Chief*. New York: Hyperion, 1996.

DiNunzio, Mario R., ed.*Theodore Roosevelt: An American Mind, Selected Writings*. New York: Penguin Books, 1994.

Donald, David. *We are Lincoln Men*. New York: Simon & Schuster, 2003.

Donovan, Robert J. *John F. Kennedy in World War II*. New York: Fawcett Publications, 1961. PT 109.

Durant, John and Alice. *Pictorial History of the American Presidents*. New York: A.S. Barnes and Company, 1955.

Esopus. No 4. Journal published biannually by The Esopus Foundation Ltd., Spring 2005.

Ferling, John & Lewis E. Braverman. "John Adams's health reconsidered." *William and Mary Quarterly*, 3rd series, 1998. LV(1):83-104.

Flexner, James Thomas. *Washington: The Indispensible Man*. Boston: Little, Brown, 1974.

Freud, Sigmund & William C. Bullit. *Woodrow Wilson: A Psychological Study*. Boston: Houghton Mifflin, 1967.

Garrison, Webb. *A Treasury of White House Tales*. Nashville: Rutledge Press, 1989, 1996.

Gilbert, Robert E. *The Mortal Presidency: Illness and Anguish in the White House*. New York: Basic Books, 1992.

Hatch, Alden. *Young "Ike": The Exciting Story of Dwight D. Eisenhower, the Farm Boy Who Became President*. New York: Washington Square Press, 1969.

Kitman, Marvin & Gen. George Washington. *George Washington's Expense Account*. New York: Grove Press, 1970.

Mazlish, Bruce. *In Search of Nixon: A Psychohistorical Inquiry*. Maryland: Pelican Books, 1973.

McCullough, David. *John Adams*. New York: Simon & Schuster, 2001.

McPherson, James M., ed. *To the Best of My Ability*. New York: DK Publishing, 2001.

Menand, Louis. *The Metaphysical Club: A Story of Ideas in America*. New York: Farrar, Straus and Giroux, 2001.

Millard, Candice. *River of Doubt : Theodore Roosevelt's Darkest Journey.* New York: Anchor Books, 2006.

Montgomery-Massingberd, Hugh (ed). *Burke's Presidential Families of the United States of American*. 2nd ed. London: Burke's Peerage Limited, 1981.

Morens, DM. "Death of a President." *New Engl J Med*. 1999: 341;1845-1849.

O'Toole, Patricia. *When Trumpets Call: Theodore Roosevelt After the White House*. New York: Simon & Schuster, 2005.

Pendergrast, Mark. *For God, Country, and Coca Cola: The Unauthorized History of the Great American Soft Drink*. New York: Basic Books, 2000.

Reynolds, Charles B. *The Standard Guide to Washington*. Washington: Foster & Reynolds, 1900.

Roosevelt, Franklin D. *F.D.R. His Personal Letters: Early Years*. New York: Duell, Sloan, & Pearce, 1947.

Sandburg, Carl. *Lincoln Collector: The Story of Oliver R. Barret's Great Private Collection*. New York: Harcourt, Brace and Company, 1950.

Sandburg, Carl. *Abraham Lincoln: The Prairie Years and the War Years, One-Volume Edition*. San Diego: Harcourt Brace Jovanovich, 1954.

Shenk, Joshua Wolf. *Lincoln's Melancholy: How Depression Challenged a President and Fueled His Greatness*. New York: Mariner Books, 2006.

Schlesinger Jr., Arthur M. *The Imperial Presidency*. Boston: Houghton Mufflin Company, 1973.

Smith, Ira R. T. & Joe Alex Morris. *Dear Mr. President.* New York: Julian Messner Inc., 1949.

Trudeau, GB. *The President Is a Lot Smarter Than You Think: A Doonesbury Book.* New York: Popular Library, 1973.

Vidal, Gore. *Lincoln: A Novel.* New York: Ballantine Books, 1984.

Vidal, Gore. *The American Presidency*. Chicago: Odonian Press/ Common Courage Press, 1999.

Voss, Frederick S. *Portraits of The Presidents: The National Portrait Gallery*. Smithsonian Institution, Washington D.C. and Rizzolia International Publications Inc., 2000.

Vowell, Sarah. *Assassination Vacation*. New York: Simon & Schuster, 2005.

Wead D. *All the Presidents' Children: Triumph and Tragedy in the Lives of America's First Families*. New York: Atria Books, 2003.

Wicker, Tom. *Kennedy without Tears: The Man beneath the Myth.* New York: William Morrow & Company, 1964.

Online

americanrevolution.org. Art Gallery Foyer. "George Washington by Gilbert Stuart." The California Society of the Order of the Founders and Patriots of America. n.d. Web. 4 Sept 2011. <http://www.americanrevolution.org/washstu.html>

Bianco, David. "A Gay White House?" *Gay Essentials* (Alyson Publications). PlanetOut.com History. <http://www.planetout.com/news/history/archive/whitehouse.html>

Burstein, Andrew. *The Passions of Andrew Jackson*. Alfred A. Knopf, February 2003. Powells.com. Excerpt from Chapter One: "The Formative Frontier." Web. 4 Sept 2011. <http://www.powells.com/biblio?show=0375414282&page=excerpt#page>

Campbell, Helen. "The Legend of a Mountain Girl and her Baby." Hanks Census & Marriage Index. *melungeons.com*. Wise, Virginia. n.d. Web. 4 Sept 2011. <http://www.melungeons.com/articles/mar2005.htm>

Castel, Albert. "Andrew Johnson." *Profiles of U.S. Presidents: Washington—Johnson*. n.d. Web. 4 Sept 2011. <http://www.presidentprofiles.com/Washington-Johnson/Johnson-Andrew.html>

Coates, Sr., Eyler Robert, ed. *The Jefferson Bible. The Life and Morals of Jesus*. n.d. Web. 4 Sept 2011. <http://www.angelfire.com/co/JeffersonBible/jeffintr.html>

Doctor Zebra, ed. doctorzebra.com. *Medical History of American Presidents*. n.d., Web. 4 September 2011. <http://doctorzebra.com/prez/>

Grant, Ulysses S. *Personal Memoirs*. New York: C.L. Webster, 1885–86; *Bartleby.com*, 2000. <http://www.bartleby.com/1011/>

Green, Peter H.R., MD, "Was JFK the Victim of an Undiagnosed Disease Common to the Irish?" *History News Network*. November 25, 2002. Web. 4 Sept 2011. <http://hnn.us/articles/1125.html>

Hand, Manus. "Benjamin Harrison's Obituary [from page 1 of the *New York Times*, March 14, 1901]." n.d. Web. 4 Sept 2011. <http://www.classicalmusicproject.com/history/obituaries/harrisonben.html>

Hand, Manus. "Calvin Coolidge's Obituary [From page 1 of The New York Times, January 6, 1933]." n.d., Web. 4 Sept 2011. <http://www.diplom.org/manus/Presidents/jcc/jccobit.html>

Hand, Manus. "Frequently Asked Dead Presidents Questions: How Did Each Dead President Die//" *Diplom.org*. n.d. Web. 4 Sept 2011. <http://www.diplom.org/manus/Presidents/faq/causes.html>

Hand, Manus. "Frequently Asked Dead Presidents Questions: What Were The Dead Presidents' Last Words??" *Diplom.org.* n.d. Web. 4 Sept 2011. <http://www.diplom.org/manus/Presidents/faq/last.html>

Hawthorne, Nathaniel. "Chapter 1: His Parentage and Early Life." *The Life of Franklin Pierce*. Ticknor, Reed and Fields, 1852. Eldritch Press On-line Books. n.d., Web. 4 Sept 2011. <http://www.eldritchpress.org/nh/fp01.html>

Holmes, David L. 2005. "The Religion of James Monroe." *The Virginia Quarterly Review*. Feb 2, 2006. Web. 4 Sept 2011. <http://www.southernhistory.net/index.php?name=News&file=article&sid=9617>

H.P.-Time.com, J.C. "Medicine: The Last Illness." *Time Magazine*. Monday, Jan. 08, 1973. Web. 4 Sept 2011. <http://www.time.com/time/magazine/article/0,9171,910536-1,00.html>

Gillespie, Veronica. *Theodore Roosevelt on Film*. The Library of Congress. American Memory. [Versions of this article appeared previously in the January 1977 issue of the *Quarterly Journal of the Library of Congress* and in *The Theodore Roosevelt Association Film Collection: A Catalog.*]. <http://memory.loc.gov/ammem/collections/troosevelt_film/trffilm.html> and <http://memory.loc.gov/ammem/collections/troosevelt_film/>

Johnson, Lady Bird. "Selections from Lady Bird's Diary on the assassination. November 22, 1963." *PBS.org*. Produced by MacNeil/Lehrer Productions and KLRU–Austin. 2001. n.d., Web. 4 Sept 2011. <http://www.pbs.org/ladybird/epicenter/epicenter_doc_diary.html>

Kosdrosky, Michael A., "Harry S. Truman." *The Res Publica*, v4n1 (December, 1992). Ashbrook Center for Foreign Affairs at Ashland University. Web. 4 Sept 2011. <http://www.ashbrook.org/publicat/respub/v4n1/kosdrosky.html>

Lloyd, Carol. "Was Lincoln Gay?" *Salon.com*. May 3, 1999. Web. 4 Sept 2011. <http://archive.salon.com/books/it/1999/04/30/lincoln/index.html>

McMillan, Joseph. "Theodore Roosevelt and Franklin Delano Roosevelt, 26th and 32nd Presidents of the United States. The Arms of Theodore Roosevelt. The Arms of Franklin Delano Roosevelt." *American Heraldry Society*. 2007. Web. 4 Sept 2011. < http://www.americanheraldry.org/pages/index.php?n=President.Roosevelt>

Miller Center of Public Affairs. "American President: An Online Reference Resource." *millercenter.org*. University of Virginia. 2007. Web. 4 Sept 2011. <http://www.millercenter.virginia.edu/index.php/Ampres/essays/johnson/biography/1?PHPSESSID=26e23b01f9cef8923e51d0606c4ea574>

"Nixon 'was on drugs.'" *BBC News*. Monday, 28 August 2000. Web. 4 Sept 2011. <http://news.bbc.co.uk/1/hi/world/americas/899916.stm>

Omim.org. *Online Mendelian Inheritance in Man*. n.d. Web. 4 September 2011. <http://omim.org/entry/600224>

Paulson, George, "Illnesses of the Brain in John Quincy Adams." *Journal of the History of the Neurosciences*, Volume 13, Number 4. December, 2004. Taylor and Francis Ltd. <http://www.ingentaconnect.com/content/tandf/jhin/2004/00000013/00000004/art00003>

PBS.org. "Lady Bird Johnson: Portrait of a First Lady. Section III At the Epicenter." n.d. Web. 4 Sept 2011. <http://www.pbs.org/ladybird/epicenter/epicenter_documentary.html>

Roosevelt, Theodore. *The Strenuous Life; Essays and Addresses*. New York: The Century Co., 1900. Copyright, 1900, by the Outlook Company; 1900, by the Churchman Co.; 1899, by the S.S. McClure Co.; 1900, by the Century Co. The DeVinne Press; *Bartleby.com*, 1998. Web. 4 Sept 2011. <http://www.bartleby.com/58/>

Roosevelt, Theodore. *Through the Brazilian Wilderness*. New York: Charles Scribner's Sons, 1914; Bartleby.com, 2000. <http://www.bartleby.com/174>

Shenk, Joshua Wolf. "The True Lincoln." *Time Magazine*. Sunday, Jun. 26, 2005. Web. 4 Sept 2011. <http://www.time.com/time/magazine/article/0,9171,1077281,00.html>

Snopes.com. "The Curse of Tucumseh." n.d. Web. 4 Sept 2011. <http://www.snopes.com/history/american/curse.asp>

Stephens, MJ., "Herman Newticks Speaks: Tecumseh's Curse." *citizine.org*. June/July 2003. Web. 4 Sept 2011. <http://www.citizinemag.com/commentary/commentary-0308_madjoy.htm>

Stewart, Marsha. "Death by Blackness." *Warren G. Harding (1865-1923)*. n.d. Web. 4 Sept 2011. <http://warrengharding.net/DEATH-BY-BLACKNESS.html>

Taylor, Tom. *Our American Cousin, A Drama, in 3 Acts*. The Project Gutenberg. Release Date: February, 2002 [Etext #3158]. Web. 4 Sept 2011. <http://www.gutenberg.org/files/3158/3158-h/3158-h.htm>

Tecce, J. J. "Body Language in 2004 Presidential Debates: President George W. Bush and Senator John F. Kerry. First Debate—September 30, 2004." *social-engineer.org*. Boston College. n.d. Web. 4 Sept 2011. < http://www.social-engineer.org/wiki/archives/EyeMovement/EyeMovement-2004ElectionAnalysis.htm>

Theodore Roosevelt Association. "Life of Theodore Roosevelt." Chartered by Act of Congress 1920. *TheodoreRoosevelt.org*. n.d. Web. 4 Sept 2011. <http://www.theodoreroosevelt.org/life/lifeoftr.htm>

Thompson, Hunter S. "HST Says Farewell: He Was a Crook." *CounterPunch*, Cockburn, Alexander and St. Clair, Jeffrey, eds. February 21, 2005. Web. 4 Sept 2011. <http://www.counterpunch.org/thompson02212005.html>

Time Magazine U.S. "Retail Trade: The Little King." *time.com*. 12 Dec 1955. Web. 4 Sept 2011. <http://205.188.238.109/time/magazine/article/0,9171,711904,00.html>

TomPaine.commonsense.org. "The Other Buchanan Controversy: Was the Fifteenth President of the United States Gay?" Oct 15 1999. Web. 4 Sept 2011. <http://tompaine.com/Archive/scontent/2458.html>

Ward, Ferdinand. "General Grant as I Knew Him." *Ulysses S. Grant Homepage.* 2006. Web. 4 Sept 2011. <http://www.granthomepage.com/intward.htm>

Wicker, Tom. "Richard Nixon, Character Above All." Excerpt from book by same name. *pbs.org,* n.d. Web. 4 Sept 2011. <http://www.pbs.org/newshour/character/essays/nixon.html>

wikipedia.com. "List of Presidents of the United States," *Wikipedia, The Free Encyclopedia,* n.d., Web. 7 Oct 2007. <http://en.wikipedia.org/w/index.php?title=List_of_Presidents_of_the_United_States&oldid=162750237>

Williams, Charles Richard, ed. "Chapter XI: Married and Prosperous-Cincinnati, 1852-1854." *The Diary and Letters of Rutherford B. Hayes.* The Ohio Historical Society. 1922. Web. 4 Sept 2011. <http://www.ohiohistory.org/onlinedoc/hayes/chapterxi.html>

Wilson, Douglas L., Davis, Rodney O., eds. *Herndon's Informants, Letters, Interviews, and Statements about Abraham Lincoln.* 2007. Web. 4 Sept 2011. <http://durer.press.uiuc.edu/wilson/html/6.html>

"Zapruder's Film of the JFK Assassination." *BBCnews.co.uk.* Web. 17 September, 2011. H2G2. <http://www.bbc.co.uk/dna/h2g2/A72491385>

TALL, SLIM, & ERECT:
AN AFTERWORD

Louis Marx (1896-1982) was known as "the Henry Ford of the toy industry." The company that bore his name was, at its height in the 1950s, the largest toy company in the world. One of his great successes was a line of Marx Miniature Figures. "Have you all of them?" the packaging succinctly asked. Described in contemporary Marx catalogs with such vital attributes as "lifelike," "sculptured," "washable," "unbreakable," and "action" (not grammatically appropriate but more accurate than "unbreakable,") the complete selection included "generals, religious, royalty, cowboys, Indians, Disney, comics, soldiers, knights, sports, and animals." But Marx's crowning achievement was his set of U.S. Presidents.

Some time in 1953, Marx decided he wanted to impress and honor his old friend Dwight Eisenhower, who had just become president. He chose to do this by memorializing him and his predecessors in injection molded plastic. Sculpted by the Ferriot Brothers out of Ohio and mass produced in one of Marx's twelve factories, the presidents stood 60 millimeters tall (about 2 3/4 inches) and were made in a white, unpainted resin. Each figurine bore the president's name on the front of the base and his number and the dates of his term on the back. They were released in a complete set of 33 or as five chronological 7-figure subsets including a second pose of President Eisenhower and two versions of First Lady Mamie Eisenhower. A miniature version of the figures (about 1 1/2 inches tall) was also produced and sold with build-it-yourself models of either the White House or the U.S. Capitol building. Some sets even came with five "Hobby Color" paints, a brush, and detailed instructions on how to "Paint Your Presidents."

Marx prepared for the end of Eisenhower's term by making prototypes of both his vice president, Richard

Nixon, and his 1956 Democratic opponent, Adlai Stevenson. Both figurines were made in small quantities and have appeared on the collector's market, as has a 1960 "candidate" pose of John F. Kennedy. Nixon and Kennedy eventually found their way into the complete set when they were elected president in their own right (Kennedy did get a new head sculpt, however, and he was joined by a pose of First Lady Jacqueline Kennedy).

At some point during the Kennedy administration, Marx began producing the figurines in a painted version, using facilities in Hong Kong. After Kennedy's assassination, Lyndon Johnson was added to the set. Alternative poses exist of George Washington, Abraham Lincoln, Franklin Roosevelt (2), Eisenhower (2), Johnson, and Nixon. Six unsuccessful candidates were also made in small quantities; two poses of Barry Goldwater in 1964, and Robert Kennedy, Charles Percy, Ronald Reagan, Nelson Rockefeller, and George Romney in 1968. A much larger number of 1968 Democratic nominee (and then-vice president) Hubert H. Humphrey were produced in tandem with the Republican nominee Nixon figurine because that election was simply too close to call, though Marx was himself a Nixon supporter. (Another piece of trivia: Marx's daughter, Patricia, married military analyst Daniel Ellsberg whose leaking of "The Pentagon Papers" seriously damaged Nixon's credibility, much to Marx's chagrin.)

In 1972, the Marx Toy Company was sold to Quaker Oats which eventually sold the Marx properties to a British concern that filed for bankruptcy in 1980. Marx himself died soon after and the toy assets have changed hands several times since then including an incarnation called "Marx Toys and Entertainment" which produced both reissues of classic Marx Toys and headlines when several corporate officers were indicted by the Securities and Exchange Commission for stock price manipulation. Unfortunately, except for the 1968 candidate Reagan figurine, the presidential line ended for Marx with Richard Nixon.

For the record, the set photographed for this book includes the most popular versions of each figure, though not necessarily the earliest. Tens of thousands of these individual figures and sets were sold in the 1960s and 70s. They were positively ubiquitous, selling in toy stores and hobby shops, as service station and supermarket premiums, and through mail order ads in national magazines.

Today, thanks to so many children who simply weren't interested enough to even take their presidents out of their cellophane bags, hundreds of sets change hands yearly on eBay, most of them in excellent to mint condition. Toy collectors, educators, presidential memorabilia fanatics, and other compulsive sorts scour the listings to find the sets in their most complete form and nicest condition; the best preserved packaging; the accompanying booklets; the Styrofoam display stands; as well as the pose variations, the errors, and even the factory prototypes (I have a metal 1968-vintage nameless figurine in my collection that could be a vague likeness of well-known Senator Eugene McCarthy or a good likeness of the vaguely-known SenatorGeorge Smathers).

Yet for all, there is still the distant but persistent call of the Marx logo, "Have you all of them?" For more than a generation the answer has always been "No." We don't have Gerald Ford, Jimmy Carter, Bill Clinton, either George Bush or Barack Obama. We have not them all.

Heaven knows I've done my part, re-sculpting the heads of the 1968 candidates to make custom versions of the missing post-Nixon presidents. Humphrey became Ford; Romney to Bush; Clinton from Rockefeller, etc. Anyone with a little patience, some modest sculpting talent, an interest in learning latex rubber molding and plastic resin casting, and an all-consuming drive to complete a childhood toy set would have done the same. Fortunately, for hundreds of fellow obsessives who bought copies of these figurines from me, I did it first so they didn't have to.

Yet, whether you believe in only the canonical 36 or in my humble additions, to fit that last golden base into the numbered Styrofoam slot is a proud and even patriotic sensation. To stand over this hallowed Hall of Presidents is to know a legion of the most significant and accomplished of collectibles for, among toy soldiers, this a veritable and venerable army of commanders-in-chief. Within their ranks and beyond, they truly stand tall, slim, and erect.

– Patric Verrone

ACKNOWLEDGMENTS

Big thanks to Teresa Carmody, Vanessa Place and everyone at Les Figues Press for publishing the unpublishable. Ben Ehrenreich, Patric Verrone, for their words, Amadou Diallo, for his prints, Victoria Welling, for her assistance, Michael Russem, for his early encouragement, to the communities of Blue Mountain Center, Ucross Foundation, and Djerassi Resident Artists Program for their support of this project, and to Fractured Atlas for their sponsorship.

Portions of *Tall, Slim & Erect* have appeared in the magazines *archipelago.org, drunkenboat.com,* and *Jubilat. Tall, Slim & Erect* was exhibited at David Krut Projects, the Derek Eller Gallery, The Matzo Files, Abrons Art Center, among others.

Special thanks to Renee Stahl Dektor, Rachel Moresky, Coleman Hough, Ofelia Ortiz Cuevas, Harriet Barlow, Ben Strader, Issa Van Dyk, Bernard Friedman & Leslie Hyatt, Michael Teig & Michelle Markley, Hans Soderquist, Matthea Harvey, Joshua Wolf Shenk, Erin Soros, Jen Hofer, Carolina Gomma Azevedo Domingues, Christian Hawkey, Michael Hawkey, Sasha Wizansky, Maria Seferian, Jack Lerner, Katherine McNamara, Joel Agee, Kate McCrickard, Agnes Berecz, Andrea Cote, Joelle Jensen, Dan Torop, Justine Kurland, Anthony Lacavaro & Athena Devlin, Carmen Einfinger, Betty Makonnen, Julia Michaels, Andrew Rubin, Gray Palmer, Jonathan Tasini, Chris Kline, Mark Landsman, Rachel Carpenter, Ross Wisdom, Peter & Jane Schneider, Mariana Ochs, Peter Seidler, Schecter Lee, Bruce Davidson.

Especially warm thanks to my family, in particular Mitch Nollman, Stacey Riegelhaupt, Ed Riegelhaupt & Pat Morrill, Ilana & Armando Strozenberg, Ephim Shluger, Tatiana Sol Shluger, Sophia Shluger, Shep & Leona Forman, Kris Jackson & Jacob Forman.

My gratitude to Louis Marx & Company and to the writers, historians, teachers, curators, researchers, and collectors of things presidential.

Alex Forman presently lives in Rio de Janeiro with her favorite hero, Ulysses, whom she named after Joyce, after Grant, after Tennyson, after Shakespeare, after Dante, after Homer, and with whom she shares "zeal ... / T'explore the world." She is a photographer, writer, editor, translator, and personal historian.

Patric M. Verrone is an Emmy-winning television writer for shows including *The Tonight Show with Johnny Carson, The Simpsons,* and *Futurama*; a Harvard-educated attorney and president of the Writers Guild of America, West; and a collector and creator of miniature historical figurines.

Ben Ehrenreich is the author of the novels *Ether* and *The Suitors.*

TrenchArt : Recon Series

6/0: TrenchArt : Recon
aesthetics

6/1: Negro marfil
Ivory Black
by Myriam Moscona (trans. Jen Hofer)
Poetry: Each color contains its opposite, each presence its absence: how might silence be inverted into speech?

6/2: Tall, Slim and Erect
by Alex Forman
Pictures & Prose: Portraits of the first 37 presidents of the United States built around Marx Toys figurines and appropriated facts and rumors.

6/3: By Kelman Out of Pessoa
by Doug Nufer
Prose: A literal experiment in the laboratory of a racetrack.

6/4: The Phonemes
by Frances Richard
Poetry: A consideration of particles of matter and particles of sound.

From Mexico to Brazil to the United States
by Renee Petropoulos
Visual: Graphic and abstract representations of individual texts and national systems of identity.

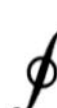

Les Figues Press
Post Office 7736
Los Angeles, CA 90007
www.lesfigues.com